Public Library Services for the Poor
Doing All We Can

Leslie Edmonds Holt | Glen E. Holt

American Library Association
Chicago   2010

Dr. Leslie Edmonds Holt is president and CEO of Holt Consulting and associate editor of *Public Library Quarterly*. She received her BA from Cornell College, her MLS from the University of Chicago, and her PhD in Education (Reading) from Loyola University. She has twenty-five years of experience working in public libraries, including a decade-long term as director of Youth Services and Community Relations at the St. Louis Public Library. She has taught at the Graduate School of Library and Information Science at the University of Illinois at Urbana-Champaign.

Dr. Glen Holt is the editor of *Public Library Quarterly*. He wrote quarterly columns on library economics in *The Bottom Line: Managing Library Finance* for eleven years and columns in *Library Leadership Network Commons* for five. In addition, he is coauthor of three LIS books and author of more than a hundred articles on library topics. In 2003 he received PLA's Charlie Robinson Award for innovation and risk taking in the profession, and he is one of only two dozen library professionals who helped articulate library best practices as a member of Germany's Bertelsmann Foundation's International Network of Public Librarians.

Library of Congress Cataloging-in-Publication Data
Holt, Leslie Edmonds
    Public library services for the poor : doing all we can / Leslie Edmonds Holt and Glen E. Holt.
        p. cm.
    Includes bibliographical references and index.
    ISBN 978-0-8389-1050-4 (alk. paper)
    1. Libraries and the poor—United States. I. Holt, Glen E. II. Title.
Z711.92.P66H65 2010
027.6—dc22

                                                                    2009045798

ISBN-13: 978-0-8389-1050-4

Printed in the United States of America
14 13 12 11 10   5 4 3 2 1

To Lowell A. Martin and Herbert Goldhor, whose clearheaded
and thoughtful professional contributions continue to
drive both theoretical and applied research in library and
information science

[As library educators,] we see our role in this field not as theorists or pioneers but as intermediaries between . . . the innovators and . . . the practitioners. We . . . utilize whatever means are open to us to translate theory into terms which are meaningful to the librarians in the field.

Herbert Goldhor, ed., Proceedings of the 1964 [University of Illinois] Clinic on Library Applications of Data Processing

[In this book, I] set down notable events in public library development . . . [and] probe for underlying trends that either furthered or deterred the growth of the institution. . . . The aim is not solely to praise the growth and success of the institution, but also to note problems and uncertainties . . . , to show the public library when it hit and when it missed.

Lowell A. Martin, *Enrichment: A History of the Public Library in the United States in the Twentieth Century*

Contents

Preface

PUBLIC LIBRARY *Services for the Poor: Doing All We Can* addresses the immediate needs of policy makers and line practitioners charged with delivering library services to the temporary and chronically poor.

The book is published during a profound economic shift in U.S. society. Through the past two decades, this nation has experienced a relative decline in the wealth held by its historic middle class and an increase in the number of families who are poor. The winners in this redistribution are the very wealthy. The political turmoil that we are currently experiencing is one manifestation of this huge change.

Public libraries are caught in these shifts. The massive economic shifts have brought many and varied demands for information, reading, and literacy services to public libraries. Institutional responses might have been quicker if public libraries had not been in a real-dollar income decline since at least 2002.[1]

LIBRARY LITERATURE ABOUT SERVICES TO THE POOR

Along with this rationale derived from shifting economics, this book's character is shaped by the shortage of prior research designed to improve library services to the chronically and temporary poor. We approached ALA Editions to publish this book because we recognized a need for a unified book-length treatment of how public libraries could improve the quantity and quality of public library services to their increasing numbers of poor constituents.

Our search for a helpful literature on how libraries should serve the poor began when each of us began our tenure at St. Louis Public Library. Since both of us came from academic backgrounds, we sought out the professional literature that would help us establish, offer, and evaluate our successes in providing library services to the poor. From the standpoint of practitioners, that literature is at best disappointing.

Most reports of library services to the poor are synopses or cryptic overviews about "how our library is going to serve the poor with this new grant" and "how we did it best." These picaresque accounts usually come with minimal details and without any mention of qualitative or quantitative evaluation of user adoption. Nor do they analyze the broader impact of the innovation on the community whose taxpayers are the primary funders of libraries. Once announcements of the new programs appear, their story line is lost. Follow-ups occur only by research on individual library websites, contact with previously unidentified staff, or references found in the invaluable electronic Internet files of local newspapers.

There have been a few prior collections of essays on library services to the poor, such as editor Karen Venturella's outstanding *Poor People and Library Services* (1998),[2] but no recent attempt by one or two authors to write a unified monograph. We review some of the best recent literature on aspects of library services and poverty in chapter 15, and other literature is cited throughout this book.

This brief discussion helps explain the subtitle of this book: "Doing all we can" suggests that U.S. public libraries can do a lot—in many cases, a lot more—to assist the chronically poor and working poor as they deal with the essential economic issues of their lives.

"Doing all we can" begins with respect—for individuals as inherently valuable because of their humanity and their past, current, or potential contributions to society. Librarians demonstrate respect when they take time to learn about the rich and often intricate cultures organized by people in poverty. Such learning needs to be based on the willingness to listen, to interpret, and to undertake research. This integrative effort to match library services to constituent needs is very different from approaching the poor as archetypical "experts" who offer instant "library solutions" to change something that seems weird about poor lives from an outsider's viewpoint.

Reiterating the same thoughts another way, we believe that successful library work with poor individuals and families requires a degree of intentionality, proactivity, and attentiveness that has seldom been demonstrated by our national government, much less by the nine thousand public library systems awash in the perils (and the opportunities) of their own localism. We hope that our book makes librarians' work with poor constituents more productive and more beneficial to the poor, to public libraries, and to society generally.

AUTHORS' EXPERIENCE

The primary basis of the book is experience, our combined thirty years developing and operating programs and services for the poor at St. Louis Public Library. In our old, highly segregated, midwestern industrial city, this library's core constituency is predominantly poor, as it has been for at least two generations.

In addition, both of us worked with the poor and working poor in our "other careers." We both have been university teachers, administrators, and independent consultants. We each have worked with, researched, written about, and provided policy advice to universities, foundations, government agencies, Head Start projects, historical societies, museums, and libraries for many different purposes. Establishing and improving programs for poor constituents often have been a significant part of these assignments.

Both of us chose to work in St. Louis as much because of its poor population as because of the vanities broadcast by the city's boosters or the resources promised by the library's board members. Unlike most of the foreign-born refugee newcomers and the multitude of second- and third-generation poor (those who are poor through the accident of birth), we were not in St. Louis because we had to be but because we wanted to be. We each came in the hope of doing good work for the people of St. Louis and for the St. Louis Public Library.

We confess this point of view in our introduction so that you know at the outset that we both saw and still see ourselves as agents of change. We have written this volume to improve the quality of library services to the poor. We believe that such work is important, not just in bad economic times but all the time. And we hope that readers find much that they can use to improve the library services of their public library districts and consortia as they consider the policy implications of this book.

Notes

1. Robert Molyneux, "Squeeze Play: Public Library Circulation and Budget Trends, FY1992–FY2004," *Public Library Quarterly* 26, nos. 3/4 (2007): 101–108.
2. Karen M. Venturella, ed., *Poor People and Library Services* (Jefferson, N.C.: McFarland, 1998).

Part I
Think and Plan

ONE

A Library Commitment to the Poor

PUBLIC LIBRARIANS need to understand how poverty levels are defined. Different agencies that provide information or partnership organizations with which your library may collaborate use various poverty standards. When your organization undertakes research on your poor constituencies, you may have to adjust national or state poverty standards to match local conditions. Such adjustments are frequently criticized when economic issues about employment and poverty make it into public policy discussions. Identifying or defining the poor locally is the first step in designing library services for low-income citizens.

DEFINING WHO'S POOR

Poverty is an economic condition: persons and families are poor when they lack money to buy goods and services. Throughout this volume, when we use the words *poor* or *in poverty*, we are referring to such persons.

New federal poverty levels are published each year at the end of January. The 2009 federally defined poverty levels in the forty-eight contiguous states and the District of Columbia are

- For a single person, a monthly income of $902.50, or $10,830 annually
- For a family of four, $1,837.50 monthly, or $22,050 annually

The federal definition of poverty was created by a staff member in the Social Security Administration in 1964. It was based on multiplying by three the U.S. Department of Agriculture's estimate of food costs for an average family in 1959. Each year the numbers are adjusted against shifts in cost-of-living figures.[1]

Many government program administrators use the current federal statistical standard of poverty by applying a multiplier to the base figure. For example, children qualify for free school lunches paid for by the federal government if their family income is no more than 133 percent of the federal poverty guideline.

Naturally, there is disagreement among individuals and organizations over the amounts that constitute poverty. Some advocacy organizations for the poor, for example, think that individuals and families need an income of about twice the federal poverty level to cover basic expenses. Using that definition, the number of those living in poverty, of course, would double.[2]

Librarians should be comfortable with this variability, because many terms in their own operational domain have a similar fuzziness. When you read any account that mentions a basis in the official definition of poverty, remember that in reality the figure is an estimate, and that officials adjust that figure on a regular basis.

DIFFERENCES IN HOW STATES DEAL WITH POVERTY

One other element that librarians will do well to know is how their state governments deal with poverty. The differences begin in the state-to-state variations of cost-of-living estimates. At minimum, the variation is hundreds of dollars per month (see table 1.1).

Furthermore, policies on how the poor are treated vary greatly from state to state. In a small town in Kansas, where faith communities regard charity as a religious imperative, or in a large city in Minnesota, where state officials legislate to assist the poor in a relatively generous way, there is quite an array of government and charity services to help the poor: senior centers and Meals on Wheels, Goodwill and Salvation Army shelters, well-stocked food banks and homeless feeding stations, church holiday baskets, and local law enforcement officials who may know and treat poor offenders by name and with respect.

In such states, it may be possible for a single oldster to live on a widow's Social Security check, occasional credit from local stores, and income from babysitting, taking in some ironing, or cleaning houses. The same woman trying to maintain the same standard of life in an urban center in another state, one that prides itself on "limited charity" for its poor, even when receiving the same categories of charity, may need to earn twice or three times as much.

Differences in states' policies about help for persons in poverty can be seen initially in cost-of-living indices. St. Louis, Missouri, in the first quarter of 2009, had the fifth-lowest cost of living (index = 96) in the nation. California indexed at 110 and Maine at 117, both among the highest.[3] State and local governments often adjust income qualifications for services to

Table 1.1
2009 POVERTY GUIDELINES ($)

Persons in Family	48 Contiguous States and the District of Columbia[a]	Alaska[b]	Hawaii[c]
1	10,830	13,530	12,460
2	14,570	18,210	16,760
3	18,310	22,890	21,060
4	22,050	27,570	25,360
5	25,790	32,250	29,660
6	29,530	36,930	33,960
7	33,270	41,610	38,260
8	37,010	46,290	42,560

Source: 2009 Poverty Guidelines for the 48 Contiguous States and the District of Columbia; 2009 Poverty Guidelines for Alaska; 2009 Poverty Guidelines for Hawaii. Tables from *Federal Register* 74, no. 14 (January 23, 2009): 4199–4201.

[a]For families with more than 8 persons, add $3,740 for each additional person.

[b]For families with more than 8 persons, add $4,680 for each additional person.

[c]For families with more than 8 persons, add $4,300 for each additional person.

allow for geographic variations in living costs, but they also may adjust definitions of poverty downward to reduce the acknowledged financial needs of the poor to fit the budget realities created by the politics of parsimony or by revenue shortfalls.

A CRITIQUE OF POVERTY STANDARDS

Critiques of poverty standards sometimes are longer than technical definitions of poverty. Expert critiques are important, however, since they often lead to revisions and help those who use poverty terms know what they are talking about. A current and quite justifiable critique of poverty standards comes from the Columbia University–based National Center for Children in Poverty:

> ### WHY IS THE CURRENT POVERTY STANDARD INADEQUATE?
> The current poverty measure is flawed in two ways.
>
> The current poverty level—that is, the specific dollar amount—is based on outdated assumptions about family expenditures.
>
> [First,] food now comprises far less than a third of an average family's expenses, while the costs of housing, child care, health care, and transportation have grown disproportionately. Thus, the poverty level does not reflect the true cost of supporting a family. In addition, the current poverty measure is a national standard that does not adjust for the substantial variation in the cost of living from state to state and between urban and rural areas.
>
> More accurate estimates of typical family expenses, and adjustments for local costs, would produce a substantially higher poverty threshold.
>
> [Second,] the method used to determine whether a family is poor does not accurately count family resources.
>
> When determining if a family is poor, income sources counted include earnings, interest, dividends, Social Security, and cash assistance. But income is counted before subtracting payroll, income, and other taxes, overstating income for some families. On the other hand, the federal Earned Income Tax Credit isn't counted either, underestimating income for other families. Also, in-kind government benefits that assist low-income families—food stamps, Medicaid, and housing and child care assistance—are not taken into account.[4]

THE POOR MAY BE OTHER THINGS

There is another complication to working with poor persons, especially highly visible groups like the homeless: often individuals and even elected officials tend to associate noneconomic social pathologies with persons in certain income categories. Like other income categories, such as "middle class" or "rich," those who are poor or in poverty may be unemployed, underemployed, single parents, latchkey kids, homeless, mentally ill, physically ill, addicted to gambling, lacking in interpersonal or work skills, overweight, undernourished, addicted to drugs or alcohol, convicted felons, practicing pedophiles, chronic "flashers," abusive in relations with others, sexually or psychologically abused by others, prostitutes, parolees, new immigrants, pitiful because of recent tragedy, visually dirty, vermin ridden, contagious disease carriers, or nauseatingly smelly. Or not, as the case may be.

Any of these other conditions distorts patterns of family life—including influencing whether or not and how individuals use their public libraries. That is because these conditions—just like being poor—influence human behavior, and therefore how people approach a library-using experience.

LABELS AND CATEGORIES

Two different practitioners, one a teacher-administrator, the other a librarian-library scholar, provide a sense of the power of a single word when someone is called "poor."

The first usage involves the stigma of the words *poor* and *poverty* noted by Sister Gail Trippett, Sister of St. Joseph of Carondelet and, until mid-2009, principal of the Central Catholic/St. Nicholas School in the heart of the city of St. Louis. This "mission school" is adjacent to a large public housing complex. Sister Gail warns teachers, volunteers, and visitors alike that within the school's walls they will not hear the word "poor." She says,

> The first breach to a child's dignity is to teach them they are poor. . . . If people say the word "poor" they often think of someone who is not intelligent, not self-activating, doesn't have dreams and won't accomplish much in life. When we label a child as "poor" that child begins to assume the myth that goes along with that word.[5]

A famous, now-deceased educator, Wendell Wray, provides a different perspective on the word *poor.* Wray borrowed this quote from cartoonist

Jules Feiffer to start a 1976 *Catholic Library World* article titled "Library Services to the Poor: Implications for Library Education":

> *I used to think I was poor.*
> *Then they told me I wasn't poor, I was needy.*
> *Then they told me it was self-defeating to*
> *think of myself as needy. I was deprived.*
> *(Oh, not deprived, but rather underprivileged.)*
> *Then they told me that underprivileged*
> *was overused. I was disadvantaged.*
> *I still don't have a dime. But I have a great vocabulary.*[6]

Wray uses Feiffer's words to proclaim that, although social conventions of naming change, the reality of being poor remains. This situation exists in libraries because all staff members have value opinions about the poor and how their institutions ought to be involved with them.

WHY WE USE THE TERM POOR IN THIS BOOK

Some librarians prefer to handle poverty with euphemisms, which—as Feiffer and Wray show—usually conceal as much as they reveal.

One of our grandfathers was fond of telling a story about euphemism, which he called "perfumed language." The story concerned one of Grandfather's friends, who had a father who had been hung as a horse thief. The friend, Grandfather said, remained sensitive about this hanging, and never more so than when he was filling out an application for life insurance. On that form, of course, was the standard question, "How did your father die?" After some thought, Grandfather's friend answered this way: "Father died when he fell from a platform while attending a public event."

That's euphemism. And that's perfumed language.

Following Wray's admonition, we stick with using the term *poor* in our book title and write about library services for the poor rather than use terms with different and fuzzier nuances. Like Sister Gail, we do not characterize poor children in negative personal ways. We do, however, believe that libraries ought to handle the matter of poverty openly—as a matter of policy and operations (see more on this point in chapter 2.)

As the authors of this volume, we encourage library professionals to face poverty head-on in their institutions. Acting as if poverty is invisible or nonexistent only obscures its reality and the real action libraries ought to take to deal with it.

Notes

1. U.S. Department of Health and Human Services, Frequently Asked Questions Related to Poverty Guidelines and Poverty, http://aspe.hhs.gov/POVERTY/faq.shtml.
2. National Center for Children in Poverty, Child Poverty (2009), www.nccp.org/topics/childpoverty.html.
3. State cost-of-living information from www.costoflivingbystate.org.
4. Sarah Fass, National Center for Children in Poverty, Measuring Poverty in the United States (May 2009), www.nccp.org/publications/pub_876.html.
5. Jeanne Liston Barnes, "The Power Within," *Connections* (issued semiannually by the Sisters of St. Joseph of Carondelet), Fall/Winter (2008): 3. Most back issues of this publication are available on the order's website at www.csjsl.org.
6. Wendell Wray, "Library Services for the Poor: Implications for Library Education," *Catholic Library World* 47, no. 8 (1976): 328–332. The corrected quote (Wray omitted the parentheses in the quote) is from http://thinkexist.com/quotes/jules_feiffer/. The quote is attributed to Feiffer in several other Internet sources as well. The Wray article is reprinted in *Public Library Quarterly* 28, no. 1 (2009): 40–48. Line breaks added by authors for reading clarity.

TWO

Ambivalences about Poverty

PEOPLE EXPRESS ambivalence when they hold two opposing ideas, attitudes, or emotions at the same time. Because the practice of librarianship deals with a mix of uncertainties about change, personal belief, professional credos, and interpersonal community service, its professionals often find themselves ambivalent, sometimes to the point of inaction. This chapter explores the societal, professional, and political ambivalences that hinder library services to poor persons.

MORAL AND ETHICAL AMBIVALENCE ABOUT POVERTY

Because the United States developed within a Judeo-Christian heritage, a good place to begin an examination of ambivalence about poverty is in the Christian Bible.[1] One of the most frequently expressed notions about poverty in the Christian Bible is its inevitability: "The poor will always be with you," proclaim both John 12:8 and Matthew 26:11. Helping the poor, meanwhile, receives desultory reviews. Mark 14:7 notes, "For you always have the poor with you, and whenever you wish you can do good to them."

Moving from the Bible's ethical commentary to television and radio's pop culture, where public figures are paid to say mean things, it is little wonder that professional commentators attribute malicious motives to the poor. An example can be found in the remarks of well-known talk-show host Bill Cunningham, who is listed in *Talkers Magazine* on its "Heavy Hundred" list of the "100 most important radio talk show hosts in America." In his nationally syndicated, October 23, 2008, radio broadcast, *Live on Saturday Night, It's Bill Cunningham,* he proclaimed, "The reason people are poor in America is not because they lack money, it's because poor people in America lack values, character, and the ability to work hard." Four days later Cunningham added, "Among the so-called noble poor in America . . . [b]irth control is not used so illegitimate children can be brought into the world, so the mom can get more checks in the mail from the government." And on the next program Cunningham asserted, "Unlike many countries in the world, . . . we have fat poor people. We don't have skinny poor people. Ours are fat and flatulent."[2]

This derisive attitude toward poverty finds its way into contemporary political leadership. Missouri state legislator Cynthia Davis, in a regular 2009 electronic newsletter to her supporters, attributes dark motives to government programs that provide children subsidized meals. "Hunger can be a positive motivator," writes Davis, who chairs the Missouri House's Special Standing Committee on Children and Families. The program to provide children with lunches and snacks in summer feeding programs for poor kids, she says, is an excuse "to create an expansion of a government program." Meanwhile, a May 2008 survey by the charity Feeding America notes that one of every five Missouri children qualifies for free or subsidized school lunch programs, tying Missouri with Louisiana as the seventh-highest state in the nation in this poverty category.[3]

"CLOSED AREAS OF THOUGHT" YIELD AMBIVALENCE

If you believe, as Cunningham and Davis do, that the poor are poor because they deserve it, you do not have to give the topic any more intellectual or ethical consideration. Lots of people do that. To use a phrase from a couple of social scientists, Maurice Hunt and Lawrence Metcalf, writing forty years ago, such areas ruled by belief rather than by rational policy debate are "closed areas of American thought."

Hunt and Metcalf warned teacher trainers and teachers that the United States had an assortment of "closed areas of thought" that were sources of trouble in school classrooms, especially social studies classrooms where curriculum planners expected teachers to deal with "value issues." These topics involved issues with so many ethical and policy crosscurrents that adult Americans simply did not want to talk about them with their families, their friends, and certainly not people (i.e., the poor) who were not successful members of the broad "middle class" like they were.[4]

According to Hunt and Metcalf, closed areas of American thought included "power and the law; religion and morality; race and minority-group relations; social class; sex, courtship, and marriage; nationalism and patriotism; and economics." Poverty and the conditions of the poor are central to all economic and social class issues and therefore involve a minefield that teachers cannot avoid but need to tiptoe through with great care because all involve latent controversies that might turn hot and dangerous for them and their schools.[5]

Hunt and Metcalf could have included "libraries" among the venues where such minefields threaten. If librarians look at the Hunt and Metcalf categories, they will recognize all the broad subject areas that have made book-banning fights a central theme in the life of their profession. Hunt and Metcalf provide no solace from attacks by persons who hold beliefs different from those revealed in the book selections and policies that librarians make as part of library management. Citizens often attack books not because of what they know but because of what they believe, to paraphrase these scholars. Thought—rational thought—may not be involved. Such citizens attack because they perceive that librarians are assaulting their closely held belief systems, and they resist every challenge to those belief systems.

Closed minds lead to ambivalent speech. Here are some examples of the extraordinarily ambivalent proclamations that we as Americans make about our nation and the facts on which they rest:

> What other nation has leaders who brag, "We have the best medical care system in the world," even though 46 million persons (18 percent) under the age of 65 do not have access to that "best system" and resort to self-diagnosis and over-the-counter remedies, "clinic medicine," or emergency-room "charity medicine." And even when they get outstanding medical care in emergency rooms, there remains the problem of follow-up care, for which most poor have little ability to pay. Moreover, the percentage of uninsured has risen steadily in the past decade.[6]

> In this "best educated" of all nations, with its abundance of high-paying jobs critical to family social and economic status, in some cities 32 percent of young persons ages 18–24, those just entering the job market, are not

employed. Our parenting, schooling, and other youth socialization activities seem incapable of meeting the educational needs of all of the nation's children and certainly not the poor among them.

In this "best-housed" nation, we express our beliefs by spatial segregation. We do not want the poor living near our homes, children's schools, social gathering points, shopping centers, or workplaces. In the United States, the poorest (who have the least control over their residences) and the wealthiest (who have the most control) are the most segregated populations in the nation.

Finally, in this "wealthiest-ever" nation, 18 percent—or nearly one in five children under 18—live in households with incomes below the federally defined poverty line.[7]

More than any other rich society in the world, the United States treats its poor with ambivalence—creating legal, social, and economic systems that operate to make the poor invisible to all of us who are not poor. As an ALA staff member told one of us recently, "Most people want to hand you a single check for $25 and then walk away believing they have done enough to help the poor for that year."

THE PROFESSION'S AMBIVALENCE ABOUT POVERTY

Mirroring national ambivalence, the library profession officially holds poverty at arm's length. Policy 61 is the ALA canon around which the profession is to organize to serve the poor. According to Sanford Berman, who advocated and cowrote the material that became the policy, the canon came into existence only with turmoil, delay, and lobbying.[8] Here are Policy 61's 145 words, last revised in 1990, which, alas, was nearly two decades ago; the world of wealth and poverty has shifted hugely in those nearly twenty years.

> The American Library Association promotes equal access to information for all persons, and recognizes the urgent need to respond to the increasing number of poor children, adults, and families in America. These people are affected by a combination of limitations, including illiteracy, illness, social isolation, homelessness, hunger, and discrimination, which hamper the effectiveness of traditional library services. Therefore it is crucial that libraries

recognize their role in enabling poor people to participate fully in a democratic society, by utilizing a wide variety of available resources and strategies. Concrete programs of training and development are needed to sensitize and prepare library staff to identify poor people's needs and deliver relevant services. And within the American Library Association the coordinating mechanisms of programs and activities dealing with poor people in various divisions, offices, and units should be strengthened, and support for low-income liaison activities should be enhanced.[9]

These five sentences can be parsed as follows: The United States has an "increasing number of poor" who are hampered by "limitations. . . . [These limitations] hamper the effectiveness of library services." Libraries should do all they can, including training staff, to help the poor. Meanwhile, ALA will involve the poor in its activities to enhance support and get ideas for "coordination of its low-income activities."

At best, it would be difficult to lead a crusade—or even operate a library—under such a vague professional canon. Yet this is the ambiguity that public library leaders discover when they turn to ALA for professional guidance on what to do about the poor.

This professional ambiguity is complicated further when the issue of poverty is amalgamated with other ambivalence-filled topics into one ALA office. Treatment of the poor in libraries is left with ALA's Office of Literacy and Outreach Services (OLOS). OLOS issues mandates covering these library service areas:

- Adult Literacy
- Bookmobiles
- Gay, Lesbian, Bisexual, and Transgendered People
- Incarcerated People and Ex-offenders
- Older Adults
- People of Color
- People with Disabilities
- Poor and Homeless
- Rural, Native, and Tribal Libraries
- Other Outreach Areas

All of these categories are significant in the profession. Sometimes they overlap; often they do not. All deserve considerable professional attention. Serving the poor is one among many OLOS responsibilities.

The principal problem of such OLOS-style catchment areas in any bureaucracy, ALA included, is that once issues are segregated for special attention and officed as part of policy conglomerates, they often are under-resourced. This is certainly the case for OLOS, which has many different mandates, each with extraordinary complexities, huge policy significance, and an extensive policy literature much of which has been produced outside almost all library and information science research.

An important part of the attention deficit toward poverty has to do with the scale of ALA as a professional organization. ALA has a 2009 annual budget of $58,000,000 and a dance card of intentions and causes from its members so myriad as to make every issue one that probably has to be reduced to a bare bones response or a postponement until next year.[10]

THE OLOS SURVEY, 2007:
WHAT WE DO, WHAT WE NEED

The profession's ambivalence about poverty is illuminated in a recent OLOS survey. In not-for-profit organizations as large as ALA, it is an act of courage when those in leadership positions ask the membership how the organization is doing and what else is needed to make practitioners successful. In 2007, ALA's Hunger, Homelessness and Poverty Task Force (HHPTF) conducted an "external survey" of services to the poor in U.S. libraries. Drafted by John Gehner, then coordinator of the HHPTF and now an adult services librarian at the Urbana (Ill.) Free Library, and reviewed by ALA's Office for Research and Statistics, OLOS sent out the survey to its actively subscribed electronic mailing lists.[11]

Access to these lists did not require ALA membership. Undoubtedly the survey took in some non-ALA members and very probably many people who did not have MLS degrees. The OLOS survey, with its 648 voluntary respondents, however, would seem to have more policy implications than the informal "surveys" conducted on PubLib and a degree of representativeness comparable to a March 2009 survey by WebJunction on a different topic.[12] OLOS mounted the results of the survey on its web page, making it available to all ALA members, and South Carolina school librarian Lisa Geiskes, the current coordinator of ALA's HHPTF, wrote about the survey in an early 2009 issue of *Public Library Quarterly*.[13]

The most significant statistical finding came early in the survey: 65 percent, or two out of every three respondents, stated that "the poor" are a significant user constituency in their library. To twist a paraphrase of a biblical quote from earlier in the chapter, "In libraries, the poor are with us most of the time."

Next came a cluster of questions that yielded a sense of the ambivalence about poverty in the respondents. Those surveyed were asked to respond to the following: "My library identifies the poor in the following manner. . . ." The responses named the definable poor as users of public computers, community members who use meeting rooms, Head Start participants, those who fall within official federal poverty guidelines, those who receive free or reduced school lunches, and those who live near the downtown library, along with "nuisance" and "high maintenance users."

Among those answering this question, some declared that labeling their patrons was offensive. But, Geiskes notes, "100% of respondents answered the question about the numbers of poor people using their library. This suggests that although the idea of patron categorization is appalling to some, library employees who took the survey do notice economic status."

Of the respondents, 58 percent left blank a query asking what specific programs for the poor their library offered. Yet many discussed specific programs their library offered in a narrative section. Based on this set of responses and other data, it appears that institutional management in many public libraries either does not have or does not provide information about institutional policy regarding services to the poor. In the rule-oriented environment of public libraries, this constitutes a striking omission. The survey suggests that managers furnished no policy context to staff even in those libraries that offered specific services to the poor.

Half the respondents said their library was involved in a partnership to serve the poor better. For the others who were not involved in partnerships, respondents overwhelming said it was because their institution had no process to create partnerships and no official library policy promoting them.

Respondents obtained information to work with poor persons from a great variety of agencies: Head Start groups and GED programs, a variety of government agencies, and philanthropies such as the United Way and Urban League.

Part of the survey was directed toward articulating needs and desires so that respondents could operate programs relevant to the needs of the poor. Here are some highlights: 85 percent advocated more training to sensitize library staff to issues affecting the poor and to attitudinal and other barriers that hinder use of libraries by the poor. Of all respondents, 82 percent wanted help to network with and cooperate with other libraries and local agencies, organizations, and advocacy groups to develop programs and services to reach the poor. When asked whether or not they knew of any libraries successfully providing services for the poor, over 70 percent of respondents said no.

Respondents also stated their high expectations for ALA. Summarizing the survey task force's finding, Geiskes calls for ALA to clarify why service to the poor is integral to the library profession, to take a broad-based and multipronged approach to gain the attention of the profession on how it might deal with issues of economic class and poverty, and to cover this set of issues with publications on a regular basis.

There is much more in the survey finding. There are many more recommendations to the profession—and to the profession's organization, ALA. For those interested in public library services to the poor, the survey and the discussion of those who brought it into being and reported it are imperative reading. No doubt, there are issues of representativeness and statistical validity in this survey. In our account of the survey, we are careful not to generalize findings beyond what its respondents and interpreters said.

The group of professionals who responded to the survey, however, took time to speak to others in their profession. In classic sociological terms, those who responded to the survey expressed professional isolation, alienation, and anomie when it came to dealing with poor constituents. To dig out of what they regard as this cauldron of indifference, this group of staff respondents said that they want professional and institutional guidance and additional resources if they are to be expected to deliver high-quality library services to the poor.

POLITICS OF POVERTY

Another important factor affecting the quality and amount of library services to the poor is politics. Whether a library is a city or county department, an independent district helping a specific community, or a large system serving many communities, it is a public entity governed by elected and appointed officials. That means that decisions about how libraries are to serve the poor are always more or less political. And, because they utilize public funds, libraries are more or less accountable to the taxpayers who fund them.

Examples abound. Community leaders may pressure the library to participate in job creation programs or object to the homeless presence in library reading rooms. Politicians may object to a library literacy program because it calls attention to the fact that the local school district is not doing its job. The political problem may also be a passive lack of knowledge: politicians have no idea how the library serves its poor constituents, so they do not allocate funds for library programs that would help the library help those in need.

The hardest thing about being an effective public library policy maker is recognizing that every decision has a political manifestation. Any director who does not pay attention to library community relations, including politicians, runs into trouble quickly. It is important to acknowledge that serving the poor may also bring political conflict—that is, some politicians support spending for library services to the poor and others oppose it. Skillful negotiations between political camps may be required for the library to move forward with services to the poor. Poverty is political because both the haves and the have-nots recognize that allocations of public funds involving programs that help or discipline the poor have implications that show up on election day.

What you as a public library practitioner or decision maker need to recognize as you move forward to develop and deliver services to the poor is that your effort is going to get somehow, somewhere, in some way, into somebody's consequential bailiwick of political issues involving power, patronage, funding, resource sharing, and taking credit for doing good works. When you effectively serve the poor, you have to be ready for local politics.

To conclude, in the United States poverty is ensnared in ambivalences. If we who operate libraries intend to provide high-quality library services to poor persons, we need to break through those ambivalences. Complicating this process, because they are human and U.S. citizens, librarians are ambivalent. Public libraries reflect and refract what is happening in their nation, state, and locale. Like all members of this society, we are caught in the ambivalence of what to say and do about the poor.

What must librarians do to cope with this "closed area of thought" and overcome ambivalences to make service to the poor a core feature of public library operations? Explicit and implicit answers to these questions fill the chapters that follow.

Notes

1. Sandie Butler et al., *The Poverty and Justice Bible: Contemporary English Version* (Stonehill Green, Westlea, Swindon, U.K.: Bible Society, 2008). Of the 31,000 total verses in the Bible, 2,848 passages and partial verses provide ethical commentary on issues of poverty and justice: 2,130 are in the Old Testament and 718 in the New Testament.
2. Widely reported on and checked against many other electronic sources, these quotes were downloaded from http://mediamatters.org/mmtv/200810290010. The quotes have never been denied.
3. Oblivious to the Needs of Missouri's Hungry Children, www.stltoday.com/blogzone/the-platform/published-editorials/2009/06/oblivious-to-the-needs-of-missouris-hungry-children/. The source of the quote, Davis's electronic newsletter, is available at http://cynthiadavis.net/PDFs/cpr090604_Summer_Food_Program.htm.
4. Maurice P. Hunt and Lawrence E. Metcalf, *Teaching High School Social Studies: Problems in Reflective Thinking and Social Understanding*, 2nd ed. (New York: Harper and Row, 1968).

5. Ibid., 26–27.

6. Carmen DeNavas-Walt, Bernadette D. Proctor, and Jessica C. Smith for the U.S. Census Bureau, "Income, Poverty, and Health Insurance Coverage in the United States: 2007" (Washington, D.C.: U.S. Government Publication Office, August 2008), www.census.gov/prod/2008pubs/p60-235.pdf. This fact is reported and interpreted in context by the National Coalition on Health Care: Facts on Health Insurance Coverage, www.nchc.org/facts/coverage.shtml (retrieved October 2009).

7. This statistic is one of many family poverty indicators compiled and arrayed by the Kids Count Data Center, www.kidscount.org.

8. Sanford Berman, "Foreword," in *Poor People and Library Services,* ed. Karen M. Venturella (Jefferson, N.C.: McFarland, 1998), 2–6.

9. American Library Association, Policy Manual, www.ala.org/ala/aboutala/governance/policymanual/servicespoor.cfm.

10. The place to start any analysis of ALA activity is its annual financials, which are clearly reported online. For the 2009 expense and income estimates, see www.ala.org/ala/aboutala/governance/annualreport/annual report/financials/financials.cfm#ala_expense.

11. The survey was based on a 1996 survey reported in Frances Smardo Dowd, "Homeless Children in Public Libraries: A National Survey of Large Systems," *Journal of Youth Services in Libraries* 9, no. 2 (Winter 1996): 155–165.

12. The WebJunction survey is reported at www.webjunction.org/voices/-/articles/content/63290797.

13. Lisa Geiskes, "Why Librarians Matter to Poor People," *Public Library Quarterly* 28, no. 1 (2009): 49–57. The quotations in this section are from this article.

THREE

Doing Our People's Work

THIS CHAPTER explains that provision of high-quality services to poor persons is a significant part of how public libraries thrive as essential institutions in the lives of their constituents.

MAYOR DALEY: WHY PUBLIC LIBRARIES ARE ESSENTIAL TO CHICAGOANS

Chicago mayor Richard M. Daley is his father's son. Like Dad (Richard J. Daley), Richard M.—after his father the second-longest serving mayor of the Windy City—lives and breathes politics. Unlike his father, however, the current Mayor Daley is a great fan of public libraries. His backing is basic, unswerving, and involves heavy financial support—which is the real test of whether politicians "like" libraries. Moreover, Daley recommends the library connection to his voting constituents. He sees his libraries as essential community institutions.

Speaking to an Urban Libraries Council conference in 2005, the mayor explained why public libraries are essential to Chicagoans (emphasis added).[1]

I really believe that *education* should be the highest priority of society and government.

The only way to improve the quality of life in America is . . . through *education,* and libraries are part of the *education* system.

I'm very fortunate here in the City of Chicago to have members of the city council—over 50—and members of the library board, [and] the business community, all coming together. Since 1989, they've made a commitment to renovating or building new libraries—over 52 of them—and *now every community wants a library.*

When you invest in libraries it's *good for the community,* it's good for *education,* it's good for the *economy,* and it's good for *families.*

The *most important place in our community is a library;* it's not a mall.

Libraries today are community anchors. When we go out and dedicate a new library, it is amazing how many new volunteers we get from the community itself and how many people look at that amount of investment in a library and see what it means . . . that we're *investing that much money in the community.* They in turn say, "We're going to start investing our own time and effort in our own community."

What we accomplish is getting the *schools, both public and private,* all together to make sure children have *library cards,* to make sure their parents have library cards, make sure their business community is coming forward and having library cards. *It's really important to have a library card in our city.*

Daley's message is clear. Public libraries are essential in Chicago because they are educational institutions and anchors for community and family economic development. Not incidentally, they also are good for local politicians who support their essential work.

We share Mayor Daley's sense of the essential nature of public libraries. His unspoken mandate for Chicago's schools and libraries—their real value to the community—is that they help individuals, children, their families, and local businesses to improve. Though Daley's comments are about libraries and the whole community, his descriptions apply especially to poor people and poor neighborhoods.

Poor neighborhoods in Chicago (and elsewhere) benefit from libraries that anchor their communities and function as safe public places, provide access to job and business information and educational resources, and support students of all ages. For Daley, the essential library mission is practical and measurable (not ethereal) uplift that creates better people, an improved economy, and therefore a better city.

ST. LOUIS PUBLIC LIBRARY: DEDICATION TO ESSENTIAL SERVICES

Both of us, one hired by the St. Louis Public Library (SLPL) board of directors in November 1986, the other hired in the spring of 1990, came to new jobs in a troubled institution in a troubled city with a mandate from the city's mayor and the governing board to function as "user advocates"—not just for those who were then using the public library but for that huge mass of mostly poor adults and children in our city who were not yet users.

Our user demographic and cardholder location studies in the late 1980s and early 1990s ratified a staff mindset: most current library users were from middle-income, white families. Those who were not using library services much, if at all, were mostly poor African American and immigrant newcomers, many with basic literacy and English literacy problems.

Current demographics have become more diverse, but still with plenty of poverty. In the twenty-first century, most St. Louis kids are poor, with 80 percent of all student-age persons eligible for the Federal School Lunch Program. The population is over 50 percent black, including some newly arrived Africans adding to the number of African Americans already here. By 2006, one out of every five St. Louis citizens was foreign born, adding ethnic, newcomer, diversity to the long-term black-white split. The public schools are unaccredited and run by the state, and adult illiteracy rates are estimated to be 28 percent. Functional illiteracy in the workplace is estimated at nearly 40 percent of all adults. The community continues to register high crime statistics, with heavy drug use and dealing and its associated high murder rate. Population loss—which had more than halved the number of city residents from 1950 to 2000—stabilized by the latter year, but poverty and its related pathologies remained a principal factor in the community and in developing library services. To increase use, SLPL had to become essential. That meant we had to attract and meet the needs of poor people in more focused and more useful ways than we were doing. Serving the poor was our best hope of boosting library use and support. It was, in fact, our only hope.

ASSETS

We had three big assets on which to build: money, technology, and public expectation.

Money

In 1988 and again in 1994, St. Louis taxpayers, irritated with the library's lackluster performance on their behalf, accepted the arguments of the institution's advocates when we made specific campaign promises about how we would use increased revenue to improve their library services. In two referenda, the voters increased the library's annual tax take from their pocketbooks from $6 million to over $16 million, a huge victory in a city where 40 percent of all participating voters vote no on any tax increase— with a negative pride that edges into braggadocio.

Technology

Technology was changing fast. St. Louis voters knew enough about the condition of their libraries and about telephones and computers to know that their libraries and library services needed big technological improvements. Of course, voters wanted more new books, but what they really spoke up for—especially during the second campaign in the early 1990s—was more computers in their neighborhood branches, computers for both children and adults. And they wanted the computers to complement, not supplant, their "regular" library services built around paper collections and programs. They wanted help from staff who were not only friendly but knew what they were doing. Moreover, they wanted a clean and attractive environment (nothing expensive or fancy, we were warned) in which to compute and to gather and to take their children to get books and help with reading and homework.

We took to heart the words of California educator Clark Kerr, who advised his university colleagues in the 1960s, "We are all caught up in the frantic race to remain contemporary."[2] Like many other public libraries at the time, SLPL was a "behind" institution. Technology offered a visible, transformational lifeline with which to build our national reputation while measurably improving the quality of services to our users. Like Kerr's university libraries in the late 1960s, U.S. libraries since the mid-1980s have had opportunities to improve their quality and performance on a scale not seen since their period of inception or some "golden age," whenever that might have been for particular systems.

Our rearticulation of Kerr's statement on higher education for libraries became "Public libraries must change in order to keep up with a world that features continuing communications technology innovations, rapidly changing ideas and new knowledge and upward mobility as the proudest testaments of the nation's progress."[3]

Public Expectation

Through the prior twenty years, a huge shift in thinking about government responsibilities had closed asylums and orphanages, cut back funding for educational institutions from kindergartens through graduate schools, and invoked a new culture-of-results measurement that cut through funding agencies from the smallest local government to the largest foundation.[4]

This latter point about accountability is hugely significant, more because of what the profession left undone than what it did. Even when the federal government legitimated measurable accountability for those who accepted any federal funds with a 1993 law, the Government Performance and Results Act, public libraries helped a private entrepreneur publicize a pseudo-measurement culture to mark out "the best" libraries rather than develop carefully delineated and reliable measurement standards to assess the quality of their work.[5] Because of that wrongly directed move, public libraries have been playing accountability catch-up for at least a couple of decades.[6]

Along with this revolution in expectations about accountability, two other grim changes took place in this country. The first, quite simply, was that as the rich grew richer, the poor grew poorer. To quote *Nickel and Dimed* author Barbara Ehrenreich's newest book, *This Land Is Their Land,* "Since 1979, the share of pretax income going to the top 1 percent of American households has risen by 7 percentage points, to 16 percent. At the same time, the share of income going to the bottom 80 percent has fallen by 7 percentage points."[7]

The middle class has not done too well either. Ehrenreich writes, "According to the Fed[eral Reserve], average inflation adjusted family incomes dropped by 2.3 percent between 2001 and 2004, to $70,700. The median family income (the point that half the families are above) rose only slightly to $43,200, and the big difference between the median and average reflects how skewed the income distribution is."[8] One of Ehrenreich's overall interpretations of what has been happening economically in the

United States can be seen in one of her section titles: "Strangling the Middle Class."

What all those articles about how libraries are busier than they were during the "bubble economy" fail to note is that in real-dollar income middle-class, working poor, and chronically poor families are poorer now than they have been for perhaps two decades. The implicit (and sometimes explicit) assumption in these proclamations is that citizens use public libraries more when economic times are tight. If that is true, then what, if anything, have libraries done to focus their services on those who are poor or at least poorer both now and in the future?

IMPROVEMENT: THE ST. LOUIS MISSION

As one of a number of old Rust Belt cities, St. Louis experienced this downward shift in family income pressure before other newer cities did. And because of its two dedicated tax increases in 1998 and 1994, SLPL became a legatee institution to which puzzled officials and civic leaders turned as they looked for help to solve the severe problems of a population segregated heavily by residence, race, ethnicity, and income.

Proactive and positive response to the immediate and most pressing needs of current and potential users is what makes public libraries essential to their society. The board of directors told the administrators of SLPL to make the institution essential to the city's residents.

SLPL has a long history of serving the poor. Started as a charity movement in 1865, the institution's operation was taken over by the schools. In 1893 the system broke free of the schools and became an independent taxing district. Not much later, Andrew Carnegie handed St. Louisans a check for $1 million to construct a main library and several branches. From these buildings and other locations, SLPL gave considerable service to immigrants and performed high-visibility service during both world wars.

The library did yeoman work for its poor and unemployed constituents through the Great Depression of the 1930s. Its beneficial tactics were well recognized among larger public libraries, including opening "extension sites" in popular stores so that city residents could check out books without riding the streetcar, driving, or walking long distances.

In the late 1940s, the city's huge downturn began, with population and tax base both shrinking rapidly. Library cuts and closings started and did not end through the 1970s and the first half of the 1980s. Deferred maintenance became a way of life, as did reductions in collection budgets and leaving important positions vacant or filling them with less than fully qualified professionals.

After twenty years of hard times and slipping backward, a new mayor appointed a new reform-oriented library board, who hired a new director with the mandate to move the institution forward. Both of us were brought to St. Louis to take a lead in that reform effort.

With more money from tax increases, the library in the late 1980s and the 1990s set a new course. Outreach beyond library walls became the way of life for professional and nonprofessional staff alike. Paint up and fix up became the facilities rule; then came new buildings or expansions and major rehabilitations of old ones. Staff increases were made as library business increased, and collection development and technology received large new inputs of money.

In the midst of this progress, the board of directors and principal administrators set out to write a new mission statement plus broad goal statements that became the basis of outcome measurements for the institution as a whole and for specific work units. That mission and goal statement, adopted in 1994, follow:

> The St. Louis Public Library will provide learning resources and information services that support and improve individual, family and community life.
>
> To support this mission, the library will organize and prudently manage its resources to:
>
> - Ensure that the library's resources are available to all.
> - Promote use of the library.
> - Assist children and adults with life-long learning.
> - Promote literacy for all ages.
> - Assist individuals in finding jobs and educational opportunities.
> - Assist businesses with their development and growth.
> - Provide current information.
> - Provide recreational reading resources, media materials, and programs.
> - Promote public use of modern information technology.

As set out by that mission and goals statement, the library's official intent was and still is to improve the lives of individuals, families, and the whole community. The goals extended the improvement theme—putting special emphasis on helping kids, businesses, job hunters, community leaders, and illiterates. Just as with Chicago Public Library under the second Mayor

Daley, SLPL set out to become the city's principal voluntary educational institution and to assist in every way possible to use public money to fuel the city's economic and cultural development.

Because of the St. Louis demographics described above, to implement the library's mission we had to figure out ways to improve the lives of poor people. We needed to find ways to help poor people to learn—and sometimes to learn to read, to use computers, and to get jobs and become successful students. What tools did we use? Books, programs, information technology, lots of outreach and marketing and high-quality librarianship—in other words, everything in our resource bank.

When we appeared before community meetings, spoke before service or economic groups, or helped orient new staff to their library work, we often invoked this kind of mission-driven litany: "What business are we in?" we asked rhetorically. Then we answered: "We proactively help people, families, and the whole community to become better than they are now. When you visit the library, we start with where you are—your question, your inability to read, your lack of time, even the fact that you don't use the library—and we work to give you help to get you exactly the reading material or the information that you want and need to make your life better. We are in the business of helping you equip yourself to earn a living or to be an effective parent. What business would you have us be in other than helping you, your family, and your community? That is intentionality. That is taking our policy cues from you, our constituent taxpayers."

FULFILLING CONSTITUENT EXPECTATIONS

To quote the title of a recent library and information science book, all of us in public libraries ought to be "questioning library neutrality."[9] Anyone who reads in the social and behavioral sciences very long recognizes that those who claim neutrality always have as strong and as vested a point of view as those who aggressively advocate particular actions for change. The maddening quality about this discussion for public librarians is that it truly is only ivory-tower academic. Our constituent taxpayers do not want us to be neutral. They want us to be for them! Even when they are mad at us, they are trying to get us to be for them.

In other words, the purposeful users and supporters of public libraries in these frightening economic times, when the philosophical relativism of "meism" has turned grayer than old clothes repeatedly and harshly washed with Grandma's lye soap, look to public libraries as agencies of "self-actualization." Libraries are not just places you go to for help; you go there for hope. The poor and the millions growing poorer want and need to learn about themselves; they need to feel successful, they need to gain optimism, and they need help to learn how to be taken seriously and to become empowered.

Serving these needs is "doing our people's work." That is the main business that all public libraries are in.

Notes

1. "Thus Said in Chicago: Mayor Daley Champions Libraries," *American Libraries* 37, no. 6 (June 2006): 27.
2. Clark Kerr, "Ex Ante—The Frantic Race to Remain Contemporary," in *The Great Transformation in Higher Education, 1960–1980* (Albany: State University of New York Press, 1991), 113–130. Originally published in *Daedalus* 93, no. 4 (Fall 1964): 1051–1070.
3. Glen E. Holt, "Library Myths That Affect Performance," *Bottom Line* 18, no. 2 (2005): 87–91.
4. See, e.g., Edward Shorter, *A History of Psychiatry: From the Era of the Asylum to the Age of Prozac* (New York: John Wiley and Sons, 1998); and Peter Barham, *Closing the Asylum: The Mental Patient in Modern Society* (London: Penguin, 1992).
5. On the statistical problems in Hennen's Public Library Index, see Ray Lyons, "Unsettling Scores: An Evaluation of Hennen's American Public Library Ratings," *Public Library Quarterly* 26, nos. 3/4 (2007): 49–100.
6. See Donald S. Elliott et al., *Measuring Your Library's Value: How to Do a Cost-Benefit Analysis for Your Public Library* (Chicago: American Library Association, 2007); and Susan Imholtz and Jennifer Weil Arns, *Worth Their Weight: An Assessment of the Evolving Field of Library Valuation* (New York: Americans for Libraries Council, 2006).
7. Barbara Ehrenreich, *This Land Is Their Land: Reports from a Divided Nation* (Evanston, Ill.: Holt McDougal, 2008), 23. The earlier book was Ehrenreich, *Nickel and Dimed: On (Not) Getting By in America* (Evanston, Ill.: Holt McDougal, 2001). On the same theme, see David K. Shipler, *The Working Poor: Invisible in America* (New York: Vintage Press, 2005).
8. Ehrenreich, *This Land,* 94.
9. Alison Lewis, ed., *Questioning Library Neutrality: Essays from Progressive Librarian* (Duluth, Minn.: Library Juice Press, 2008).

Part II
Act

FOUR

Getting Started
Principles of Success

THIS CHAPTER is the first of eight "action" chapters intended to lay out ways librarians can organize resources to integrate effective programs into the lives of the poor. This chapter provides general guidelines for taking successful action.

CUSTOMER-DRIVEN LIBRARY SERVICES FOR THE POOR

Because the United States is so ambivalent about poverty, institutions that develop poverty programs have to face the issue of whether they will operate as "supply-side" programs or "demand-driven" programs. Library supply-siders operate on the premise that there is a demand for every service they offer: no matter what you do, or how well or badly you do it, users, including the poor, will use the service avidly.

If you have already read other chapters in this book, you know that as library professionals we fit into the category of those who believe that optimal use of public funds takes place when libraries meet specific demands from their constituencies. Sometimes that demand is apparent; sometimes it is latent and has to be discovered or revealed through user research.

To put the matter in retail language, we see the public library as a set of boutiques, all with some general characteristics (just as all retailing has general shared characteristics) but with great variability in how and what attracts and satisfies customers. For all kinds of reasons, no set of users is more finicky about using the library than poor persons, and a central tenet of this book is that libraries must integrate the needed services into the lives of the poor. The following section offers some general guidelines for making that integration successful.

PRINCIPLES OF SUCCESS

Start where you are. When he spoke at the opening of the Atlanta Cotton States and International Exposition in 1895, the great educator Booker T. Washington used this anecdote to tell his listeners how to improve race relations and the economic conditions of African Americans:

> A ship lost at sea for many days suddenly sighted a friendly vessel. From the mast of the unfortunate vessel was seen a signal, "Water, water; we die of thirst!"
>
> The answer from the friendly vessel at once came back, "Cast down your bucket where you are."
>
> A second time the signal, "Water, water; send us water!" ran up from the distressed vessel, and was answered, "Cast down your bucket where you are."
>
> The captain of the distressed vessel, at last heeding the injunction, cast down his bucket, and it came up full of fresh, sparkling water from the mouth of the Amazon River.[1]

Library professionals often have asked us, "Where should we begin to serve the poor? Where should we do more?" To paraphrase Booker T. Washington's admonition, "Put down your library bucket where you are. But start. And start now."

Build on your strengths. If you are not sure of your strengths, find out what they are. A simple SWOT (Strengths/Weaknesses/Opportunities/Threats) analysis can help. So can a vision exercise. Or just talk with your current customers—and go meet with people you would like to use your institution. The work is not hard. It is just work that needs doing.

Services to the poor should be compatible with other library services. Those who engage in institutional analysis will tell you that there is no more dangerous time than when an organization is spinning wildly through untried innovations.

Assess the situation in your locale. Locate the poor in your community and assess the reading, information, and program needs and wants of your various poor constituencies. Assessment should be both quantitative and qualitative. You need to know what experts on poverty regard as the size of the poor population groups that live in your service district. You need to talk with users who have no or very few reading and information options other than your library, asking them appropriately phrased, valid questions that include real possibilities and limits for what is possible for you to do with them and for them.

Plan within your community context. Services should fit within your community's social and political parameters. St. Louis is not rural Alabama is not Los Angeles is not Phoenix is not Fayetteville or any of the smaller or larger places in between. You do not need library planning boilerplate here but facts about and opinions of those whom you ought to be serving. Here is the question that is as hard to answer as it is simple to ask: What do your poor constituencies need that your library has or can develop the professional competencies to provide?

Relate all services to mission. Services to the poor, as all services, should be mission driven. Libraries generally should not organize and operate nonlibrary services for the poor (e.g., a food pantry, a day-care facility, a shower room, a homeless shelter). If you want a good reason why not, here it is: while your institution is learning and running a new business, who will operate your library business? "We're in the library business" expresses not only a professional value but a legal reason for public library funding. In the most elemental terms, the tax money you use was approved by the voters or elected officials for the purpose of operating your library as an educational institution. The laws of your state and locale say that the public library is to do its essential library job and do it well.

Cooperate with other agencies serving the poor. You should not become a homeless shelter, food pantry, or Head Start center, but you should coop- erate with and support with library services those groups that do provide these services. Cooperation does not mean controlling your partner; it means cooperative decision making with that partner. As your bureaucracy and that bureaucracy intersect, disagreements are bound to arise. Be pre- pared for them and to work to alleviate them.

Articulate a rationale for the services you provide and the limits of your services. Define the limits of services to the poor and a rationale for why you deliver the services you provide and not other services. The library staff and the public in about equal amounts need to know the rationale, especially the rationale for what you do not and will not do. Not having the money should never be the first or only reason a library does not provide a poverty service—such a claim immediately politicizes service policy, and politicians love to hammer agencies when they get that kind of opening.

Train staff to operate the programs to achieve specified outcomes and impacts. Training needs to include not only the methods of service delivery but help in talking about library services to one or the many persons who use or do not use your library. Accountability should reign as one training principle.

Assign sufficient staff and provide other resources to make the programs successful and to sustain them. Librarians are famous for "making do" and adding more programs without much thought to what staff time, materials, and leadership are needed to ensure quality and high impact for the users. Most new programs and services are started on the fly, but to sustain robust, mature programs and services for the poor the library needs to allocate time and money.

Measure the effectiveness and impact of programs for the poor. Assure the quality of the services you provide as you provide them, and assess the impact of those services on those served and on the community after the services are delivered. These are different processes with different purposes. One is an operational assessment. The other is an impact or benefits study.

Operate within your library's legal framework. In our research and consultation, we have often found that trouble over services to the poor begins when library managers or a library board ignore the laws under which public libraries operate. Educating latchkey children, busing seniors from their retirement homes to use a library, and allowing the homeless to wash their clothes in the library restroom all are actions that take place within a legal framework that libraries are bound to follow—or to get the laws changed. A thorough reading of the Internet material on the famous *Kreimer vs. Morristown* case is well worth the time invested.[2] That case demonstrates profoundly what happens when a potential litigant involves a whole institution in a legal showdown. The network of library laws needs to be understood and observed, and the more dependent the population, the easier it is to make unintentional but costly legal mistakes in complying with these laws.

Fund programs to ensure their stability. Because services you deliver to poor persons are essential elements in their lives, as much as possible you should deliver them with stable funding from within your hard-line budget or with long-term commitments from donors or foundations. Abandoning a successful program when the grant runs out is disappointing to users. You are fundamentally disrespecting your constituents when you start and promote an attractive program, then kill it after a year or two "because the money runs out." Nothing loses your constituents faster than disrespecting them. That is probably truer for the poor than for the middle class, because most middle-class families have learned that they can negotiate for options or use an alternative. Poor people often do not have such options, and when they walk away from the library they become very hard to win back.

QUALITY WITH BALANCE

Like social work, librarianship is a helping profession, with the ability to research and organize and compile. Like business administration, it is a retail profession that works to deliver its services to the point of most immediate contact with its users, clients, or customers with efficiency and effectiveness. Like the social and behavioral sciences, it must master both methods and content—and professional content is varied and broadening. Like electronic media, librarians must recognize how fast their knowledge base is changing and how rapidly the educational, recreational, and service expectations of their users are shifting as well.

High-quality library service to any user group is always a matter of balancing resources in an optimal way. The way to begin and operate those services is with a clear vision, solid planning, appropriate resources, and a pretty solid definition about what your library will not do as well as what it will do. Start with the principles of success reviewed above and then get specific about your service situation.

Notes

1. Booker T. Washington, "Cast Down Your Bucket . . . ," from the Atlanta Cotton States and International Exposition of 1895, *Social Contract Journal* 15, no. 4 (Summer 2005), www.thesocialcontract.com/artman2/publish/tsc1504/article_1338.shtml. Extra paragraph breaks inserted for easier reading.
2. Start with 765 F.Supp 181 (D.N.J. 1991), *Richard R. Kreimer, Plaintiff, v. Bureau of Police for the Town of Morristown, et al., Defendants.* No. 90-554 (HLS). U.S. District Court, District of New Jersey, May 22, 1991.

FIVE

Getting Started

Service Continuum

IN THIS chapter we introduce the service continuum tool, designed to help libraries choose services that fit explicitly within the dual context of library work and the community environment. Libraries big and small ought to utilize explicit, rational service selection and planning. The service continuum is a simple tool to aid that endeavor.

ARRAYING CHOICES

Big public libraries often engage in elaborate planning processes. Sometimes these are so long and suck up so many resources that the opportunity to act slips by before preparation can be accomplished. Since change often comes easier in smaller organizations, small and rural libraries tend to be more informal in their planning. The negative consequence of this informality is that a change may carry implicit aberrations that are difficult to overcome. To act intentionally, plan explicitly. But recognize that planning can become a substitute for action rather than preparation for action.

We recommend the use of simple language with the service continuum tool. Services, for example, are readily categorized as Traditional, Targeted, Priority, or sufficiently innovative in the profession to make your institution a Model Builder or Leader. Similarly, it is not difficult for library policy makers to differentiate among different categories of resource types, offerings, and infrastructure categories. These possibilities are shown in table 5.1. This grid has service commitment types on the horizontal axis and library services on the vertical axis.

The designated planning team decides which level of service to the poor it should and can provide and then identifies activities in each service component that are helpful to the poor. Using the service continuum grid helps identify what the library is actually doing for the poor (or what makes it difficult for the poor to use the library) and what can be done to increase the effectiveness of the services offered. Here is more detail about the various categories in the continuum of table 5.1.

Levels of Service

Libraries operating at the *traditional level of service* offer the same set of activities and rules to all those served. Users from all income levels are welcome to use what the library offers, but no special effort is made to reach out to the poor or enhance their experiences with the library. This alternative is attractive to libraries with limited resources and may seem to be the fairest way to run the library. If the community served is affluent or there are few poor residents in the district, there would be no reason to move from traditional to targeted services for the poor.

An assessment of income levels of the whole community is essential before one can decide that traditional service is appropriate for all income levels in the community. Small libraries with few staff members may have no choice but to offer traditional services for poor people because they have no way to serve any special populations (e.g., children, business professionals, or immigrants). Librarians, however, pride themselves on tweaking services by adding a few resources—a few more books, a little extra staff time, a few more programs—to cater to particular groups within the whole.

That tweaking leads naturally into the next category on the continuum, the *targeted level of service.* In targeting, the library intentionally and explicitly organizes a few or several specific services for the poor. For example, the library might offer a program about how to apply for home loans or college scholarships available to low-income families. Except for these few targeted services, low-income and poor people would otherwise use the same services offered all users. The library develops targeted services in response to known or knowable community needs.

In an economic downturn, the library can add targeted services for the working poor and unemployed persons. The library might offer special

Table 5.1

CONTINUUM OF LIBRARY SERVICES TO THE POOR

Service Component	LEVEL OF SERVICE			
	Traditional: All incomes welcomed / Basic services	Targeted: Specific services for low-income individuals	Priority: Services to low-income individuals are a time and budget priority	Model Builder/ Leader: Meet community needs in innovative ways
A. The library has Collections Technology Facilities: Hours, signage, etc.				
B. The library provides Individual (reference, referral, readers' advisory, etc.) Programs (group activities) Community outreach				
C. The library manages Policies and rules Staff Marketing				

41

reference help for laid-off workers who need to apply for jobs online. A housing authority or agency may ask to partner with the library to get information out into the community about opportunities for home ownership. If the local high school no longer offers college counseling, the library may want to identify online and print sources of information on colleges and college scholarships and student loans and post this information on its web page. These programs may be helpful to both middle-income and poorer people, but they are intended to answer a need that is particularly heartfelt for the poor.

At the *priority level of service,* the library acknowledges that many in the community are chronically or temporarily poor and that the library needs to make financial and resource commitments over time to meet the specific needs of this large element of the constituency. There may be many reasons libraries choose to offer priority services to the poor. If your community is poor, serving the poor is a priority and every part of the library should acknowledge that priority.

Another reason that a library makes services to the poor a priority is that it has a particular population that is problematic or is not well served. If a library is regularly visited by homeless people, or the community has many services for "at risk" children and teens, it needs to adjust services to meet customer needs and to assure that the library operates well for all users. To avoid unpleasant interactions, to obey the law, and to offer consistent, high-quality service to specific poor populations, the library needs to make such service a priority. Having a plan, programs, services, and policy for the homeless, for example, will more likely bring success than ignoring their potential as valuable human beings and the pathologies that many homeless bring to the library with them.

In communities where the library is truly committed to serving low-income persons, there are opportunities to develop innovative programs and partnerships that help the poor, help the community, and serve as models to the field. These *model builders* are leaders who are successful in seeking solutions. In these libraries, there are administration and staff who are knowledgeable or who become knowledgeable about both library services and poor persons and families. These libraries have boards and a community that are willing to find new ways and new funding to help the poor. Model builders also share their successes with other libraries and other communities through publications and professional workshops.

Service Components

Service components are a summary of what the library does to serve its community. These categories help focus on how library decisions affect users and to some extent nonusers. The categories may vary from library to library, and certainly the names a library uses to describe various services can be different from those in this continuum. The idea is to cover all aspects of the library work and identify the implications for users and potential users who are poor. The continuum should be customer focused and state benefits from the users' point of view.

The first service components in table 5.1 represent things the library has, purchases, or otherwise acquires. All libraries maintain a collection of physical items for circulation or use in the library: books (audio and paper), periodicals, DVDs, CDs, and perhaps maps, toys, or kits. Another basic that libraries provide is digital technology: computer hardware, software, and wireless connectivity used in the library as well as a website, blogs, YouTube, Facebook, or Twitter services available outside the library facility. Most libraries offer access to subscription databases and indexes and an electronic catalog. Libraries also have a facility for customer use. Although facilities are the most difficult and expensive to change, how the space is managed—hours, comfort, parking, signage, and seating—can affect how well customers are served. The library's location in the community influences who uses it.

The next components are what the library provides to serve the community. In many different surveys, library users acknowledge the value they place on individual help from staff. Along with being respectful and friendly, that help includes high-quality reference, readers' advisory, referral, help with technology, as well as fair treatment of customers when enforcing library rules and policies. Libraries also provide a variety of programs or group activities. These can be educational, informational, or recreational and can be run by staff or by outside groups. Some libraries offer services outside their buildings, such as programs and bookmobile stops at senior centers, participation in college information fairs at the high school, and library staff service on a chamber of commerce or other civic committee.

The service components in the final group are infrastructure resources managed behind the scenes that affect the user's experience at the library. As public agencies, libraries have policies and rules to ensure the safe and fair operation of the library. Many communities and most states have laws that pertain to the library. Over and above the "have to" rules in federal, state, and local law, many libraries have longtime rules about what users can do and how they may use the library's resources. What rules there are, how they are enforced, and what recourse users have to complain about their treatment can affect how the library is viewed and how it is used (or not used) by the poor.

How the staff is trained, their knowledge (of content, the library, and the community), and their friendliness and manners often influence whether users want to interact with them or not and whether users have a success-ful experience at the library.

How the library markets its services and to whom directly influence what various segments of the community know about what the library has to offer and how the services work. This publicity may include fliers given out at the library and other places in the community, advertising (public service announcements, billboards, or paid advertising), or presentations to community groups. Who "gets the message" about library services affects who uses the library. As we discuss in chapter 7, we favor a program of comprehensive institutional communications to constituents rather than a retail-style "feature of the week" approach.

USING THE CONTINUUM FOR ASSESSMENT

One purpose of the continuum is to assess what services a library has that help the poor no matter the level of service. The first step of this assess-ment is to have a clear and specific description of the target population. If the continuum is being used to assess service to the homeless, the target description should include estimates of how many homeless there are in the library service area, some demographic information (gender, age, race, etc.), and what agencies other than the library provide services for the homeless. If your target is the poor in general, you likewise need to describe community (neighborhood, zip code) income levels, demographic information, service providers, and some of the issues facing the poor in your community.

Next, this assessment can be used to identify strengths and weakness or service gaps and give a "big picture" look at how the library serves the poor in general or specific low-income groups in particular. The first step in using the continuum is to list or describe specific programs and services the library offers in each category that help the poor (or more specifically, the homeless, the low literate, the elderly poor, etc.). Box 5.1 shows examples of such services. It is important to note specifically what the library has or what it does that is helpful to the poor, not to indicate an elusively general claim that the poor can read books in the collection. What in the collection will be of particular interest or help to them?

After completing this step, the library can record the level of service currently being offered. Staff can then identify gaps or changes that can be made or decide that current services need to be upgraded to another ser-vice level in order to meet the needs of the poor. There should be congruity between the level of poverty in the community and the level of services the library offers the poor. Even in communities where a small portion of

Box 5.1
EXAMPLES OF SERVICES USED BY THE POOR

Collections
Résumé/job manuals
Small adult reader (low literacy) collection

Technology
Computers/wireless connection for card holders
GED online

Facilities
Open when homeless shelter is not
Close to bus stop

Individual Services
Can help set up e-mail address and apply for job online
Staff use 2-1-1 for referral to various help agencies

Programs
Storytime for Head Start families
Tax help for low-income elderly (by outside group)

Community Outreach
Book delivery to the disabled
Storytime at community center

Policies and Rules
Day passes for computer use; library card not required
Lockers for storing belongings

Staff
Customer service training required
Language training for those who work with immigrants

Marketing
Library fliers at homeless shelters and food pantries
Library advertises on public transportation

the population is poor, the library should understand how they serve the poor and ask if there are ways they can improve that service.

Some libraries will be pleasantly surprised to identify the numerous ways they serve the poor. Other libraries will realize that their institution needs to upgrade its services to the poor because what it offers does not have the impact it should or meet the goal of the library to serve the whole community. In this case, new activities and materials would be added and less effective activities would be dropped. Before adding or dropping items from the continuum, it is helpful to first state a need or goal that the component should meet and include some evaluation of how well the activity meets the library's goals.

USING THE CONTINUUM FOR PLANNING

When using the continuum for planning, the library should incorporate whatever planning scheme it uses for its strategic or long-term planning. Some libraries use PLA's *Strategic Planning for Results* so the continuum should include community needs and library roles and goals. If the library or local government uses balanced scorecard planning, it can use environmental scans, set goals, and articulate outcomes. Many libraries are beginning to use outcome evaluation and planning, so that language can easily be incorporated into the continuum (as in table 5.2). Any format will do, just keep it as simple as possible. Remember that overly elaborate planning can slow change rather than direct it.

Of course, an individual library would have no reason to fill in all the cells in the continuum as in table 5.2. This table was part of a report for the Missouri State Library to give examples about the levels of service a library might offer to low-income and low-literacy families. This table does, however, show a range of possibilities for carrying out a particular set of planning objectives for low-income and literacy-limited families.

After a library has selected a level of service as a goal and identified services the library will provide, any changes needed can become part of an annual or strategic plan of service. The library should assign a time period for developing and providing new services as well as for dropping any service. Budget and staff should be assigned to these service activities, and some kind of systematic evaluation or assessment should be implemented so that the library knows how successful it has been in implementing changes to serve the poor better. If changes do not really improve service or are impractical or too expensive, the library should adapt or abandon the new service and try something else.

Table 5.2
FAMILY LITERACY CONTINUUM WITH OUTCOMES

	LEVEL OF SERVICE			
Service Component	Traditional: Families are welcomed / Basic services	Targeted: Specific services for families with children	Priority: Family literacy services are a time and budget priority	Model Builder/Leader: Meet community needs in innovative ways
A. Library Provides				
Technology/Computing Computers/software Websites Databases **Needs:** Patrons use technologies and the Internet to develop literacy. Patrons use technologies and the Internet to develop computing skills. Patrons use technologies and the Internet to develop information literacy.	**Outcome:** Parents and children use computers. **Strategy:** Provides public use computers. **Indicator:** Parents and children strengthen information skills using the library's computers.	**Outcome:** Low-literate families use reading skill programs via library computers/website. **Strategy:** Library identifies and makes available skill-building software/websites for use by children and adults. **Indicator:** Low-literate parents and their children improve their reading/prereading skills by using library computers.	**Outcome:** Low-literate families visit the literacy portal. **Strategies:** Library provides literacy portal for children and adults; offers computer instruction to interested patrons requesting help. **Indicators:** Patrons using technology enhance literacy skills. Patrons using technology enhance computing skills. Information literacy increases for users of the library's literacy portal.	**Outcome:** Low-literate families and groups use the literacy computer lab. **Strategy:** Library provides a literacy computer lab that can accommodate group use; provides instruction in computer applications in a variety of forms (classes, Club Tech). **Indicator:** Information literacy skills improve for users of library's literacy lab.

Source: Adapted from LSTA Literacy Service Plan Assessment Project, Developed by the St. Louis Public Library, May 2004.

The continuum should be revised every few years to keep it current with both changes in the community and changes at the library.

One more thing. Planning with a continuum of service is a great place to start thinking about assessment (how well the program is working) and evaluation (the positive impact and benefits of the program). There is a lot more on that subject in chapter 14.

SIX

What Keeps Poor People from Using Libraries?

IT IS A RARE library that does not already serve chronically (e.g., under-employed, single parent with functional literacy) or temporarily (e.g., just divorced, lost job, new baby, major health problem) poor persons as part of its regular constituencies. This chapter examines the "library culture" that poor persons encounter when they visit the library and how those elements may be perceived by those who are living and working in a "poverty culture."

All public libraries use policies, procedures, and rules to fulfill their legal and financial responsibilities to their taxpayers and other funders who support them. If these are invoked appropriately, they protect the fiduciary interests of the taxpayers and establish a broad framework for fair use by constituents. That being said, some libraries and librarians seem obsessed with order—they never met a rule they didn't like. These same professionals seem unaware of how common library practices and rules make it difficult for poor people to make use of the library.

In this chapter we offer some observations about how and why poor family members use and do not use their public libraries. We hope these observations get you and your staff thinking about how to remove barriers and compete better for the time of poor constituents and of all your other users as well.

LOCALISM

Public libraries create no greater set of poor victims than when governing agencies or boards decree that their library will serve "only the residents of our community." Localism, not fines and regular user fees, is the greatest deterrent to library use for poor persons. On their way to and from their employment, church, or school, the poor may pass by any number of libraries that have the materials they need but that will not serve them unless they pay a nonresident fee. In spite of the fact that the costs of sharing are so small that almost every state library could find some way to cover them, it is easier to let the economic segregation of localism prevail. The poor suffer the most from this situation; they are the least able to come up with the fees for using libraries in different political subdivisions.

LIBRARY ACTION. Educate your governance officials, including your state library, about the advantages and realities of reciprocal lending, collaborative programming, and jointly offered services. Like everyone else in our society, the poor recognize that communication, including television and the Internet, and the economy generally (i.e., jobs) have become international. In this new world reality, many expect libraries to be able to cooperate in the interests of their users. Remember that the lives the people—including many poor people—live is part of a regional, national, and world culture.

BADLY BEHAVED STAFF

One cool fall evening, the two of us visited a branch library in a southeastern coastal city. An older white woman sat at the children's reference desk. Five African American tweens quietly entered their library, all carrying school textbooks or heavy backpacks. It was obvious they did not know how to use the library. Finally, the two boys walked to the desk and one asked, "How can we find books on American history?" Without looking up from the material on her desk, raising her left hand and pointing vaguely at a broad shelf section, the staff member proclaimed in a loud voice, "They're over there!" Within ten minutes the children were gone, and the staff member still never looked up even at the two middle-aged white folks walking around her room looking at materials, displays, and her. Whenever anyone says "Libraries should treat all users alike," this is the incident we remember. Being equally rude should not be the goal. Rather, respecting users, including the poor, who may be less able and less experienced in negotiating with library staff, ought to be a service commitment.

LIBRARY ACTION. In our decade-long cost-benefit study, staff help was one of three major values that users assigned to public libraries. Being helpful is not optional; it is a requirement. And helpful means knowing enough to help a user—or to ask another staff member for help—and being respectful and friendly. Welcoming the poor to your library begins with staff training so that such service quality is a given for every visitor, phone caller, or virtual access user.

REQUIRING A LIBRARY CARD TO CHECK OUT MATERIALS OR GET SERVICES

Getting a library card and checking out materials at a library are not free. Dealing with a lean family budget often makes poor families reluctant to incur debt, even in the nickel-and-dime amounts that most public libraries charge for fines or the dollar for a reserve or first-run movie DVD rental. Many poor people have cards but are over the fine limit, so they stop using the library.

Reacting to fines and the cost of lost books, or just fearing such expenses, parents and caregivers in poor families may make a rational decision to not allow their children to get a library card or to check out books that might get lost. Hence, children may be obeying their parents or caregivers when they visit a library location to use computers, books, or magazines but refuse to get a library card or check out materials of any kind.

LIBRARY ACTION. Review and clarify your library's fine policies. Decide if and when desk staff can waive fines or fees. Some libraries create guest passes for people to use the computers (but not check out books); some libraries offer creative, or at least systematic, ways for people to pay—and work off—fines; and some define special places where kids can lounge while they read a book or magazine in the library youth area rather than check it out. Recognize that in low-income neighborhoods library fine policy is a factor in holding down circulation and any other library use requiring a valid card.

UNSTABLE RESIDENTIAL ADDRESS

Some libraries require proof of residence to get a card or guest pass. Because poor families tend to move frequently, many treat housing as a replaceable commodity. They move to stay ahead of the landlord, to get closer to family, to move away from drug traffickers or abusive relatives or partners, or to obtain even marginally better housing for about the same money. In most cities, utilities like gas, water, and telephone record the "churn rate" (the number of shut-offs and turn-ons that mark "move outs" and "move ins") in poorer neighborhoods as double, triple, or quadruple those in community areas with more expensive housing.

LIBRARY ACTION. The library policy dilemma is how to protect your taxpayers against exorbitant losses of materials with a population that may be inherently unstable. The answer is not a "scofflaw culture" where desk staff disregard registration details when issuing cards, reflected in very high error rates in cards. Rather, it is the development of a library policy that is as rationale and humane as your policy makers can make it. Without endorsing either, we know that some libraries are using credit card–backed identification and fingerprinting to deal with this issue. Some libraries use guest passes instead of cards for computer users or allow homeless to get a short-term card by using a shelter address.

LACK OF TRANSPORTATION

Not all users have cars or are within walking distance of a library. Poor and low-income people may depend on public transportation, so libraries that are located close to bus and rail stops may be easier for them to use.

LIBRARY ACTION. On their websites and in other advertising, libraries should give directions to the library that feature public transportation and nonvehicular routes. Additionally, if there is free or low-cost transportation for disabled persons or the elderly available in the community, whether to multiple locations or just to certain libraries, staff should know how that works and proactively help potential users access this resource.[1]

LIBRARY COMMUNICATIONS

How should the library communicate with those who have no constant mail address? Local, regional, and national magazine and newspaper circulation is low in poor neighborhoods. In their weakened condition, daily metropolitan newspaper advertisements have only minimal effect. Many poor families may not have a single phone number used by all family members. Prepaid mobile phones have randomized voice communications even more than they were previously, when phone service had to be turned on or shut off at a wired location. For many people who carry cell phones, especially those that are disposable, it is not unusual for different family members to have many different phone numbers or to carry more than one phone, each with a different number. Also, one family member may program all the frequently called numbers in a phone, meaning that the cell carrier/user really does not know any phone numbers; she just pushes buttons to connect with labels like "PaPa," "Aunt Em," or "Tamika."

LIBRARY ACTION. Just like other organizations, libraries need to collect e-mail addresses and ask what kind of electronic communications the person would like to have from the library. Libraries also need to use a multiplicity of communication forms to get their message to continuing or new constituent users. This communication needs to include all electronic forms used by their constituents, including cell phone and text messaging.

ILLITERACY AND FUNCTIONAL ILLITERACY

Many low-income people also have literacy issues. Most new immigrant populations by their nature have very high English illiteracy rates. Seniors, many of whom left school to work through the Great Depression, World War II, and the Korean Conflict, are often illiterate or have many literacy problems. Adults who did not graduate from high school or who went to underperforming schools may not read well. Child illiteracy is a huge problem in the United States among poor children. Agencies focusing on literacy tell us that in 2007 about 30 percent of 10- to 13-year-olds scored below basic reading level,[2] and in 2003 perhaps 40 percent of all adults were illiterate to the point of having problems functioning in the workplace.[3]

LIBRARY ACTION. How does your library communicate with low-literate and illiterate persons? Graphic information needs to supplement written notices. Spoken messages, whether electronic or in person, need to stand beside the written word. Keep messages simple and avoid library jargon. Notable examples include one library's confusing web page link box, titled "Book a Computer." Another library on its services directory sheet had a heading labeled "PACs." And, of course, there is the old and constant problem of what a library "Reference" sign means to users, especially someone who wants only directions to a restroom or copy machine. Finally, there is that ultimate mix-up over what exactly is "Special" about "Special Collections," which in one library means GLTB (gay, lesbian, transsexual, and bisexual literature), in another the papers of author Mark Twain, and in a third local historical photographs and news clippings.

A reading teacher or adult literacy worker can help you form messages that are more likely to be read by people who are not good readers. Encourage word-of-mouth campaigns by inviting people to bring a friend to the library so the more literate can help the less literate.

GOVERNMENT BUREAUCRACY

For all kinds of reasons, poor persons often perceive public libraries as another place where they will encounter government bureaucracy, not an exception to it. More than wealthier persons, they find their lives subject to rules and procedures, some of which seem unfair and even unjust from their points of view. In their initial encounters with and continuing use of the library, every member of a poor community, even those who have never used a local library, will come to have a strong opinion as to whether their community library is friendly and helpful or just one more government bureaucracy to be negotiated to get a little help. To invoke an old cliché, the poor may see libraries as "part of the problem, not part of any solution." Bureaucratic behavior is a good way to drive away poor users from libraries.

LIBRARY ACTION. Training staff to give good customer service and teaching them techniques to help poor people feel comfortable in the library are essential to success in serving the poor. Eliminating every possible bureaucratic rule is a great step forward in creating a hospitable library.

HARRIED LIFESTYLE

Living poor means a scarcity of time. Working one job is hard enough. Working two or three is grinding. Add to that the complications of finding and keeping dependable child care or helping out sick family members without any financial reserves to meet such crises. It should be no mystery, then, why the poor end up distracted—worrying about where they have to be next, or tomorrow, or how to get to a store before it closes or church before the service is over—when they are trying to work or relax or sleep. Part of this compromised lifestyle is meals eaten at odd hours or on the run or just skipped completely. Moreover, kids as young as 10 or 12 "babysit" their younger siblings and sometimes friends of their siblings even when they are trying to study, attend a library program, or make their way to and from school in buildings different from their own.

LIBRARY ACTION. Some libraries have opened coffee shops and canteens where snacks may be purchased. Others offer free snacks at after-school programs. And some recognize the babysitting problem by offering programs for different-aged children at the same time, so a tween can drop off a young sibling for storytime before attending a computer class.

FEAR FOR PERSONAL SAFETY

Personal safety is a paramount issue in many poor neighborhoods. Witness, for example, the popularity of "after-care" programs, where kids go even if the programs are not inspiring or very helpful. Poor kids may drop into the library because their other choices are limited, less pleasant, or less safe than the library. Adults may meet business colleagues, tutors, or drug counselors at the library because it is safe, convenient, and has parking. People who serve the poor may want to use library space for informational meetings because there are few public places in the community. Libraries need a good meeting room policy that allows for added services (polling place, blood pressure screening, etc.). But to avoid advocacy and "giving value" to a particular business, political group, or religion, that policy must also deal openly with issues such as businesses that want to sell, politicians who want to campaign, and faith groups that want to worship and take up collections.

LIBRARY ACTION. If libraries cannot serve as safe harbors in bad neighborhoods, how can they be successful libraries? The basis of all other library operations is personal safety for staff and for users. When professional librarians do not face this issue, their ambivalence detracts from every other aspect of their library business, especially for those populations who can enter only a few public places without having an invitation or "a good reason." Library safety is far too often a "closed area of library thought." And when prospective users feel that libraries are not safe, they stay away from them.

ATTRACTIONS OF STREET LIFE

Poverty reduces options. The high-status, moneymaking options of street life offer straightforward and often quick methods of overcoming poverty for many youth and adults.

The attractions of gang life, for example, often are misunderstood by non-residents. Modern-day gang life is a powerful form of elemental and very adult capitalism with franchise control over territory in which to distribute goods and services; membership in a respected "family" of allies and even friends; and a business model featuring international and regional trade with import of high-value merchandise, wholesale distribution and retail selling, with large profits to be made every step in the process. Decades ago sociologist Daniel Bell documented how criminal gangs had always been a powerful tool for upward mobility in the United States.[4] Library managers should never forget that in poor neighborhoods many forms of competitive capitalism exist outside the doors of their institutions, in the process affecting the educational, social, and family lives on which they want to have a positive impact.

LIBRARY ACTION. Libraries work best in this sometimes-hostile but opportunity-laden culture when they function as alternative institutions that offer many options to what the young and old alike may experience in the other parts of their lives. You can see that a library is doing its job when young men, sometimes clad in gang colors, enter the library to help their younger siblings learn at library computers; when you see groups of young persons attending a library program to learn alternatives to violence; when library staff or volunteers help after-schoolers make videos to mount on YouTube; or when young mothers come to attend programs on inexpensive home decorations or bring their children on a free bus trip and visit to a suburban museum for a cooperative program in which the library is involved.

Programs like these are not only about survival right now but about aspirations for the future. Homework help is a necessity; a library Club Tech caters to aspirations. Loaning books on vegetable gardens probably caters to necessity; providing really knowledgeable information about how young men and women can get into trade schools or college deals with aspirations.

Public libraries that want to serve the needs of their poor constituents will do well to start with neighborhood and family realities that are part of the culture in which their current and potential users live and work. At the same time, library leaders need to assess the realities of the library culture they have established in their institutions. To an immigrant newcomer, for that matter to anyone who has never used a library, entering the building is a little like going into a strange institution in a foreign country. If the library culture is not only hospitable but helpful, the newcomer adapts quickly to get at what is wanted and needed. If the library culture seems hostile, eerie, or just hard to learn, it is likely that the poor person will do without, seek help elsewhere, and not return unless forced to do so.

Notes

1. For an example of special transportation to the library, see Victoria Gannon, "Residents Check Out Free Rides to Library: A Program in Scarborough Helps Seniors or Those with Poor Vision Make Good Use of the Library," *Portland Press Herald* (Maine), June 10, 2004.
2. Profile for the United States, Kids Count Data Center, http://datacenter .kidscount.org/data/acrossstates/Rankings.aspx?ind=85.
3. Mark Kutner et al., *Literacy in Everyday Life: Results from the 2003 National Assessment of Adult Literacy* (Washington, D.C.: U.S. Department of Education, NCES, April 2007), 13.
4. Daniel Bell, "Crime as an American Way of Life," *Antioch Review* 13 (1953): 131–154. A more modern treatment for a single ethnic group is Wendy H. Bergoffen, "Guardians, Millionaires, and Fearless Fighters: Transforming Jewish Gangsters into a Usable Past," *Shofar: An Interdisciplinary Journal of Jewish Studies* 25, no. 3 (Spring 2007): 91–110.

SEVEN

Communicating with Poor Constituents

THIS CHAPTER proposes a series of methods both typical and unusual by which libraries can communicate effectively with poor persons and families, all as part of an institutional communications program.

COMMUNICATION FOR WHAT

Librarian-scholar Taylor Willingham writes, "Public and community-based leaders must think entrepreneurially." She continues:

> Libraries connect people with information, are vital to democracy and transform communities. Led and staffed by entrepreneurial thinkers, many libraries have reaffirmed their civic mission and even redefined their role in their community. They are not only relevant to their community; they are central players in engaging the public in civic discourse, weaving organizations and resources together, bridging divisions, and developing the capacity for their communities to solve problems. These libraries are places where people learn about complex public issues

and practice deliberative democracy. By listening deeply
to the concerns of people in their community, library staff
are actively developing strategies to help the community
work together.[1]

Willingham wonderfully articulates the consultative role of public libraries within their communities. Along with consultation, the other half of the
library communication equation is presentation of programs and services
that extend the library's civic reach to attract constituent use. In communicating with poor constituents, library leaders need to pay particular
attention to educating the illiterate, to helping people recognize how they
can use library services to improve themselves and their families, and to
broadening their appeal to the unserved by helping them learn about the
free services the library offers.

Library communication is not like retail merchandising, selling first one
thing, then another. Library communication, instead, is a prolonged and
ongoing conversation, with librarians reshaping and reiterating services
that meet the wants and needs of all users, including poor persons. The
ultimate aim of library communication is to get people of all kinds, including poor persons, to use the library to improve themselves and thereby to
improve society.

FIRST COMMUNICATION CONCERN:
LISTENING RATHER THAN MARKETING

Real communication with constituents begins when professionals are sufficiently comfortable with their expertise to listen to their users and potential
users in order to find out what those folks like about the library's range of
services, what they do not like about them, what they think the experts
ought to do better—and what the institution ought to be doing that it is not
doing at all. In summary, the steps of the library communication process
are to listen, to comprehend the messages being heard, and then to respond
with policy and program changes that positively affect those who use them
and, at the same time, yield positive benefits to the whole society.

Of course, users or potential users will not express fully developed
program and service changes, and some of the constituent messages will
be garbled or posturing or malarkey. Users—especially poor users—do
not have the knowledge about library policy options that library professionals do.

Library leaders often have to wrap significant knowledge around their
constituents' ideas—knowledge about possibilities that users have not even

come close to thinking about and knowledge about the real resource limits (including the limits of librarian skill sets, building efficacy, and the priorities of other library work already under way). Within that context, however, are constituent observations that are worth their weight in library gold.

HOW DO WE COMMUNICATE ABOUT NEEDS AND WANTS?

Libraries can use lots of different communication tools. We suggest that most libraries ought to use a greater variety of them than they do. Here is a brief overview of the possibilities:

Talks with your staff and volunteers. The employees and helpers you most want in these sessions are those who have done a good job of building relationships with users—and those may be techs, clerks, librarians or volunteers. They may work inside your buildings, in outreach programs that go beyond the library walls, and they include those who run virtual services. It was such groups that informed us at SLPL in the early 1990s that we probably could never have too many public access computers, and that most of the adults and many of the children we served were going to need instruction in using computers because they were not getting that information anywhere else—certainly not at home or school.

Exit surveys with current users. The query might be along these lines: "Our library is very concerned about the number of our users who appear to be suffering from the nation's and this community's current economic problems. What services do we offer now that such persons use or might use? Are there other things we ought to do to give more help to people who are coping with hard economic issues?" In other words, individuals can speak on behalf of poor persons, not for themselves as poor persons. The questions are basic: describe and suggest changes you would like to see the library make.

Focus groups with current users and nonusers. Ask for help from day-care centers, homeless shelters, senior centers, and area businesses to find groups of individuals who don't use the library. Many will tell you that they "don't have time." This answer may be a mask for "I don't have a good reason, so I'll tell you this one." People in every income bracket prioritize their time. What about your library makes nonusers not have the time? Another masking answer is "I don't need what the library has." As with time, that may or may not be true, so follow up with a question series: "What do you read? Where do you get what you read?" Or, "Do you buy what you want to read?" And, "Do you have children? Where do you get books for them to read?" Or, "Do your kids ever ask you for more books than you give them?"

As these sequences suggest, assume that people make up answers when they don't have one, that "I don't have time" is often a made-up or masking answer. Just as important, many nonusers may not use the library because they don't know what it has or that it might be easy to use.

Conversations with current or potential institutional partners. These might include day-care providers; public, parochial, and private school teachers and administrators; homeless shelter operators; veterans' group representatives; United Way workers; and faith-based charitable volunteers. Ask them what the library could do better or do that it does not do.

Conversations with communications industry professionals. Reporters, on-air personalities, and media production staff follow story developments and help make decisions about what goes on the air. What have they seen? What would they like to see the library do or do differently?

This list is suggestive rather than definitive. The point, however, is that library communications should be based on conversations with current and potential constituents. That is as true for any user group as it is for those who are poor.

HOW TO TELL THE NONUSER POOR ABOUT YOUR LIBRARY'S SERVICES FOR THEM

After listening and thinking and planning, libraries also need to converse with poor users about what they have to offer.

Frame the communication like the service. Begin by recognizing that the service frame with poor persons is twofold. To quote the father-son consultant team of Ned and Ardy Roberto, who have been writing a regular column on marketing for more than five years for the *Philippine Daily Inquirer,* you have to segment your poor audiences. Using their terms, products or services for the poor should be "affordable" (something needed right now that they can afford with the resources at hand, e.g., time) or "aspirational" (says something about how to improve their current status or situation, or something they hope to get in the future).[2] Library planners will do well to keep this simple but profound advice in mind as they prepare programs and services for those without many economic resources.

Train staff in relationship building with customers. Training should not be used to empower amateur psychologists; there are enough of those already on every library staff. Neither should they be questions that can be construed as fishing for compliments. The sociology of "secondary associations," on which all public service librarianship is based, helps define appropriate limits and openings. Two recent books can help greatly with training in relationship building: Sara Laughlin and Ray W. Wilson's *The Quality Library,* and Edmund A. Rossman's *Castles against Ignorance.*[3]

Communicate with kids because kids lead in families rich and poor. Kids lead their parents in the selection of foods, study locations, and places that offer experiences they want to try or repeat. There are good reasons why retailers use Ronald McDonald, Mickey Mouse, Barbie, and athletic stars and music sensations to push their products. Publicize the reality that your library is a great kids' attraction and a great place for adults to come with their kids. At SLPL, we helped build our identity with children by having not one but two large community mascots, a huge nerdy, purple Theo Thesaurus dinosaur and a svelte, sleek, long-lashed, green Dina Dictionary dinosaur. Peopled by young people who worked as theme park dancers in the summer, our two figures knew all the latest dance steps and would dance with the kids and each other. We knew we had achieved the kids' visibility we wanted when, walking with our library mascots during our city's big Thanksgiving day parade, the male part of our writing duo watched an excited child cry out to her caregiver above the band music and cheers, "That's Theo, Mommy! And the green one is Dina!" The very small girl was introducing her mom to the library's representatives, whom she had met during their visit to her kindergarten. As her mother told us some time later, Theo and Dina were "the first cartoon characters that Tamesha knew personally." Tamesha had a visible symbol of the library that she could tell other kids about. Theo and Dina became part of her frame of reference, "living" symbols for the library.

Advertise on the radio stations to which the poor listen. A decade ago, SLPL chose six stations whose demographics were well matched to our library user base (e.g., black radio, sports radio, soft rock, gospel, and more recently hip-hop and rap). The radio ads were used to illustrate to listeners that the library was part of their world, and that we had tapes and later CDs of their music, books on subjects they might enjoy reading about, and movies they might enjoy watching. We found radio good for reaching the poor because their interests cut across radio demographics.

Communicate by action to improve poor neighborhoods. Start by making your library buildings safe havens in their neighborhoods. If at all possible, work with neighborhood leaders and police to close houses of prostitution and places that sell drugs that are in close proximity to the library. Both are illegal activities that cause endless amounts of trouble where they operate. True, you may not be able to do more than make these activities move from the geographic areas in which you operate, but even that change is worthwhile for the health and safety of your staff and users. Your neighbors will be endlessly grateful, and you will have done wonders to tell the whole community that your library wants to help them improve their individual, family, and community life.

Communicate on the outside and inside of public transit and on neighborhood billboards. The messages need to convey institutional credibility and appeal for use in an intriguing, friendly way.

Ask ministers in poor neighborhoods to help convey the library's positive messages. SLPL representatives met with members of the African-American Ministerial Alliance to provide them with talking points to promote the Library Summer Reading Program and the availability of public access computers at their neighborhood libraries.

Regularly visit school classrooms and leave behind talking points about library programs so the teachers will continue to act as the library's agents.

Tell the library's story through communication partners. SLPL had two big communication partners, the St. Louis Cardinals baseball club and Channel 11, an independent local television station. Libraries need to seek out partners to help insert their public service announcements on the television programs of sporting events and sitcoms that are broadly watched.

Make day-care providers partners in early childhood reading. Teaching them early childhood reading-help techniques gives day-care staff confidence at their work and encourages them to check out more library materials for the kids they care for. You also will be pleased at the number of library visits such instruction provokes.

Encourage all staff to participate in community organizations. SLPL had many staff who became officers and committee chairs in neighborhood organizations, ranging from central business district boosters to commercial and residential organizations in many different communities. These staff always took the latest library handouts to meetings so community residents could take them home.

Communicate electronically. Columbus Public Library issued its 2008 annual report only in electronic format, claiming that the library issued the document to demonstrate the following points:[4]

> To staff, public [and] stakeholders we are saying [about our electronic annual report]
> - It is green. No nonrenewable elements were used.
> - It is fiscally responsible. The whole thing cost us less than $100.
> - It is more impactful. Instead of a few thousand people having access to it, it can circle the globe. . . .
> - It is innovative. Just as we are innovative in how we deliver library service. . . .
> - It is all about discovery. Just as the library experience is a journey of discovery. . . .

Baltimore, Chicago, Hennepin County, Orange County (Fla.), and Hartford all do remarkable jobs in communicating electronically the concept that the library has help for poor persons, including immigrant newcomers.

Communicate within cell phone culture. Recent research from India shows us how profound cell phones are in the lives of even very poor persons.[5] Cell phone "primary circles" are intimate relatives and dependable friends. In poor cultures, these persons are the most likely persons from whom short-term help or relief is obtained. "Give me a ride" or "pick me up after work" are calls made as part of a poor person's resource network. So is "take care of the baby" or "stop by KFC and pick up some supper."

Whole communications businesses have grown up to find ways for private-sector businesses to break into private communication networks. Facebook and Twitter are only two of the best known of these communication mechanisms. Poor children and young adults all tend to have more access to personal cell phones than to computers.

Cell phones have created an entirely new communications culture for poor and rich alike. Libraries need to do a lot more with this culture, especially given the fact that fewer and fewer of their users have listed land-based lines. In chapter 10 we report on how elegantly a few libraries are making use of public access computers to drive their business and build their user constituencies. Technology is an ever-changing mistress, however. In other nations, ubiquitous wireless communication is far more popular than landlines, with their more expensive physical base. In the United States, cell phone–only households are growing rapidly, constituting as much as 25 percent of all families in 2009.[6]

Communicate with imaginative and functional buildings. Charlotte and Mecklenburg County (N.C.) Public Library's ImaginOn, a combined children's library and theater, is a testament to what a first-class library system can give to its constituents. Like Columbus's electronic annual report, it says "Your library system cared enough to give you users our very best." Glen Holt writes:

> ImaginOn is a building that carries out the message in its portmanteau name: Its intent is to inspire its visitors and the staff who work there to "Imagine On" both now and in the future. This building is a place that gives the people of Charlotte and Mecklenburg County a great gift: It says, "Your library and your civic officials care so much about you that they built you a library/theater where you will experience dozens of sights, sounds and feelings that will fire your imagination—where you are encouraged to ImaginOn."[7]

Go where users are electronically. ImaginOn also has special marketing features designed to appeal to preteen and teen users. The building contains video production facilities, and the ImaginOn staff has instructional capability to help the teens produce electronic programs. These in turn can be placed in the virtual worlds where kids interact with others their own age. In one example, the library teen users put ImaginOn's Loft on MySpace (www.myspace.com/libraryloft). In another, they placed ImaginOn on Teen Second Life (see www.plcmc.org/teens/secondlife.asp).

> At Second Life, ImaginOn staff have helped teen Internet users set up their own community (Eye4You Alliance Island). "Why does the library have an island in Teen Second Life?" the ImaginOn website asks. Because! "Learning how to navigate in 3D environments whether it's for online education courses (many universities and even middle schools are using second life to teach!) or participating in other events, is something the library can help with."[8]

Communicate directly, systematically, and regularly. In a city of 340,000, SLPL mails its monthly newsletter to more than 85,000 different addresses. The mailing includes all current cardholders and lots of politicians and civic leaders whom management believes need to be kept up on what is happening at the library. And inside each newsletter is a foldout calendar of all the library's programs at every library location and offsite (partnered) locations as well, along with the notation that all are open to the public. St. Louis is not the only library that does such extensive constituent mailings. Scarborough (Maine) Public Library sends monthly e-mail updates, writing that it is "introducing the next step in library service, designed to keep you up-to-date on newly published books, audio books, DVDs—whatever your interests."[9]

Why don't we use e-mail instead of bulk mail to communicate with poor families? Because so many of a library's poor constituents do not have access to e-mail at home, school, or office. Even now, the percentage of poor persons with access to Internet computers is well below the national average.

Create a buzz. To break into the complicated patterns of the lives of poor persons, libraries have to communicate repetitively through known and often-used communication venues in multiple formats. Word-of-mouth often turns out to be the best library advertising in poor neighborhoods. As a matter of good business practice, libraries need to find ways to create a buzz among families and friends about library programs that they want poor folks to attend. Contests and giveaways involving kids are one of our library's mainstays in creating a buzz about library services and programs.

Communicate effectively within library buildings. In general, visitors tend to have difficulty finding their way around public buildings. According to our architectural friends and a doctoral dissertation by Ann Beecher, there are three types of public buildings that cause more trouble than most: airports, hospitals, and libraries, all of which combine idiosyncratic design and the need for specificity rather than approximation in location—plus, all involve a high level of user stress around the desire to use time well.[10] Certainly we know from our own experiences and the kinds of directional questions our staff answers that most U.S. library visitors do not visit libraries in a leisurely way. Our buildings ought to take advantage of every opportunity to save the time of poor users and users generally.

In conducting her research, Beecher sent volunteer new visitors with small tape recorders to record their routes and reactions through three different public libraries—one traditional, one contemporary, and one modern. The study examined how architecture, layout, color, signage, computer support, and collection shelving organization affect the success of individuals as they attempt to retrieve materials and answer questions using the library. Beecher's findings are a calm recounting of how professional librarians disrespect their users when they pay insufficient attention to the interior organization of the buildings of which they are so proud. She writes:

> Many of the wayfinding tools currently available in libraries do not facilitate item retrieval. Inconsistencies, ambiguities, obstructions, disparities, and operational deficiencies all contributed to end-user frustration and retrieval failure. The study suggests that failing to address these issues may prompt library patrons—end users who are increasingly interested in finding information with minimal expenditures of time and effort—may turn to other information-retrieval strategies and abandon a system that they find confusing and frustrating.[11]

And none of Beecher's information-seeker testers were low literates or new immigrants or just a poor single mother trying to take care of a little library business on her way home from work with her latchkey kids waiting for her in the children's department.

Easy in-building wayfinding starts with crisp design and implicitly helpful spatial arrangements. These need to be aided with an organized family of signs that convey an appropriate amount of information about what to do next for visitors who are not where they want to be. When there is sensitive wayfinding help for visitors, those who are poor, like those who are rich, will enter the library to discover two important things: how their library has anticipated their essential wants and needs, and how their library respects them, values them as human beings, and seeks to build a personal relationship with them and their families. It conveys this respectful attitude by the way it helps people find what they want without asking a staff member for the simplest kind of directional help ("Where is the women's restroom?" or, "Where is 025.523?" or, "Somebody told me recipe books are in 'Cookery.' Where's the Cookery Department?")

SETTING COMMUNICATION PRIORITIES

Every phase of communicating with the poor needs to be part of your library's comprehensive communications program, which is a planned, focused effort to brand the library's core identity into the mind of its users, its funders, and those who govern it.

The problem with public libraries is that too often they are like Harriet Beecher Stowe's "Topsy" in *Uncle Tom's Cabin,* a wild and uncivilized slave girl who declared that she knew nothing about God, and that she was a creature unto herself. "I s'pect I just growed," Topsy said. "Don't think nobody ever made me." Library communication needs to go well beyond Topsy and "just growed."

As we have pointed out elsewhere in this book, libraries are like other for-profit and not-for-profit businesses in that they must have a unified focus in their work and in the way they present their image. That is as true for the multiple groups of poor users as it is for middle- and upper-class users.

As we attempt to outline in this chapter, a unified institutional communications program offers lots of different ways to communicate systematically within a comprehensive program. We hope your attention to serving the poor encourages your library to undertake such an effort at planned and effective institutional communications with them.

Notes
1. Taylor L. Willingham, "Libraries as Civic Agents." *Public Library Quarterly* 27, no. 2 (2008): 97.
2. Ned Roberto and Ardy Roberto, "Marketing to the Poor—One More Time!" *Philippine Inquirer,* August 22, 2003.

3. Sara Laughlin and Ray W. Wilson, *The Quality Library: A Guide to Staff-Driven Improvement, Better Efficiency and Happier Customers* (Chicago: American Library Association, 2008); and Edmund A. Rossman, *Castles against Ignorance: How to Make Libraries Great Educational Environments* (published by the author, 2006).

4. Columbus Public Library annual report taken from http://ourstory .columbuslibrary.org.

5. "Delhi Kids Top List of Internet, Cell Users," *International Reporter* 37, no. 10 (August 1, 2009), www.internationalreporter.com/News-5068/delhi -kids-top-list-of-internet-cell-users.html. See also Eric Bellman, "Rural India Snaps Up Mobile Phones," *Wall Street Journal,* February 9, 2009.

6. Mark Blumenthal, "Cell Phones and Political Surveys: Part 1," Pollster .com, July 3, 2007, www.pollster.com/blogs/cell_phones_and_political _surv.php.

7. Glen E. Holt, "ImaginOn: The First 21st Century Public Library Building in the US," *Public Library Quarterly* 27, no. 2 (2008): 187.

8. Ibid., 190.

9. See Scarborough's invitation to receive the library's newsletter at www .booksite.com/texis/scripts/bookletter/addnluser.html?sid=6611.

10. Ann B. Beecher, "Wayfinding Tools in Public Library Buildings: A Multiple Case Study" (PhD dissertation, University of North Texas, May 2004).

11. Ibid.

EIGHT

Finding Help for Your Poor
A Librarian's Guide

THIS CHAPTER offers a guide to sources of information that practitioners can use to get started mastering the content by which to count and ascertain the types of poverty that exist in their locale and the kinds of help that agencies and philanthropy have available for them. Such research provides a relatively sophisticated information base from which to provide information to the temporary and chronically poor.

INFORMATION THAT LIBRARIANS CAN USE TO HELP THE POOR

For several reasons, librarians need to know some of the basics of services to the poor available in their community. First, understanding the landscape for the poor in the community helps librarians understand and locate the poor. Second, knowing what is available and something about the requirements for aid prepares staff to provide accurate information to low-income library users who need help in navigating the aid system. Third, knowing what organizations and agencies provide services helps identify service partners and sometimes funding sources as the library increases its services to the poor. Fourth, if you do not have appropriate and correct information available, you may make public statements that make you sound naive or even ill informed in your advocacy.

There are three realities about the information that librarians need if they intend to furnish accurate advice to the poor about where to get help:

Lots of help exists, but it varies from state to state and locale to locale. To the credit of the people of the United States, our poor have access to help from both government and charity organizations. Those librarians who say they are in the business of helping the poor in any way have to master some of the complexities of how that assistance is allocated and distributed. They will find many distribution mechanisms. However, what services are actually available, how much help can be expected, and how easy it is to get this help vary considerably from state to state and community to community.

To help, some library staff have to master complex and detailed content. To put the matter quite simply, at least some public library staff in institutions both large and small are going to have to master the complex and sometimes arcane content of poverty programs at the federal, state, and local levels. If libraries are unwilling or unable to spend the time compiling, assessing, and arraying this kind of information, then they should be honest and refer poor persons to knowledgeable experts in nonlibrary agencies.

The most current information is available only electronically. Every book and printed pamphlet, every brochure and helpful printed checklist, is likely to be out of date—if not today, then tomorrow or the next day. The only chance your library has to keep up with information that actually helps the poor is found online—at all manner of government and charity websites. If you want to give accurate information to poor persons, your best friend is your high-speed Internet connection.

What follows is a general introduction to information available to help the poor. This information is at a fairly general level so that it does not go out of date too quickly. Nevertheless, follow the advice in the previous paragraph and check appropriate websites for recent updates.

GOVERNMENT PROGRAMS

All levels of government offer services that help poor citizens. Local governments (towns, cities, counties) tax citizens to offer services at no charge to the users. Public libraries as well as public schools, parks, some health services, and other social services are available to citizens regardless of income, but they provide basic support for the poor who cannot otherwise afford to pay for these services. Local services are regulated by local, state, and federal law as subjected to the political process and administered by assigned agencies.

Federal Programs

Federal welfare programs were begun in the 1930s as a response to the Great Depression. Most programs were administered locally by federal workers. In 1996, Congress passed and President Clinton signed the Personal Responsibility and Work Opportunity Reconciliation Act, better know as Welfare to Work. This law limited the total number of months families can receive welfare benefits and generally transferred welfare administration, including eligibility requirements, to the states. Since 1996 many fewer people are "on welfare," but other programs such as food stamps, unemployment benefits, and housing subsidies have changed and grown, depending on how each state chooses to use federal block grants and supplement these funds with state tax dollars.

The most prominent exceptions to these generalizations are Social Security, Medicare, and parts of Medicaid. These still are administered by federal agencies, although, because health care is regulated by the states, some benefits vary from place to place. Veterans' benefits are still provided by federal agencies, though again some states support supplemental programs for vets.

Confused Yet? Well, Just Wait . . .

To find out what programs are available locally, one can start with various federal Internet sources that direct you to the corresponding state's department web source, which directs you to the closest local service office. Federal websites also summarize what services are offered, who might be eligible, and often specific issues involved in providing services. Although most of the federal online sources are quite easy to use, states vary in the usefulness of their sites, including many differences in what various programs are called, who exactly they serve, and what programs are available. In addition to government information, the local or regional United Way or other umbrella nongovernment agency may provide an electronic directory of local services and staff to help navigate what is available. Most communities also have a 2-1-1 telephone service that provides phone counselors to help individuals find the help they need for programs supported by government funds. United Way often runs this service, but this can vary.

The U.S. Department of Health and Human Services is a good place to start information gathering, since many (though certainly not all) services for the poor are defined or funded by this department. Start with "Frequently Asked Questions Related to the Poverty Guidelines and Poverty" (http://aspe.hhs.gov/poverty/faq.shtml).

This site can be described as "all you want to know" about the basis for federal help for poor and low-income people. It lists about forty federal programs that serve the poor and is updated to have current information and correct citations to the U.S. Code authorizing the guidelines. Box 8.1 lists some examples of Health and Human Services programs of interest. Notice that each program passes money to state agencies with guidelines and oversight on how the federal dollars are to be spent.

Other federal agencies also have programs that serve the poor. The U.S. Department of Agriculture manages the Food Stamp Program, the National School Lunch Program, and WIC (a nutrition program for women, infants, and children). The U.S. Department of Labor offers the Job Corps, the Senior Community Service Employment Program, and the Workforce Investment in Youth Activities. Various other agencies offer help for low-rent public housing, Section 8 subsidized housing assistance, legal assistance for the poor, low-income tax assistance clinics, and support for foster grandparents. The full list of programs is long and involves many departments, bureaus, or agencies, but our list provides considerable understanding of the breadth of programs available at the federal level.

Since federal programs are funded through the annual budget voted by Congress and approved by the president, the actual amount of service offered or supported by the federal government varies from year to year. Much of the government's information is available online, including authorizing and budget documents, regulations and rules, and consumer and user information. One reason to go to federal websites is that you are likely to find more recent information there than in printed documents.

State Programs

Each state receives federal dollars for a variety of programs serving the poor. Some federal programs require some matching state dollars. States then incorporate the federal money into the state's annual budget with specifics of how the money will be spent and what state tax dollars will be used to supplement services. For example, states set income levels for eligibility for children's health insurance for the SCHIP (State Children's Heath Insurance Program). Texas, for example, sets eligibility at family income of 200 percent of the federal poverty level, whereas some states try to provide universal health insurance for children without limiting them by income eligibility restrictions. Families who have recently lost private insurance for their children may not be aware of SCHIP or know how to apply for benefits for their children.

Local Programs

County, city, and town governments get state money and either provide services to citizens or contract with organizations and individuals to

U.S. DEPARTMENT OF HEALTH AND HUMAN SERVICES EXAMPLES OF PROGRAMS FOR THE POOR

Community Services Block Grant

www.acf.hhs.gov/programs/ocs/csbg/index.html

Community Services block grants to local governments and nonprofit agencies provide a variety of anti-poverty services such as emergency health, food, housing, day care, transportation assistance, housing counseling, financial management assistance, nutrition programs including federal surplus food distribution, community gardening projects, food banks, job counseling, placement and training services, and homeless prevention programs.

Community Food and Nutrition Program

http://frac.org/html/federal_food_programs/programs/cfnp.html

The Community Food and Nutrition Program is the primary source of federal funding for anti-hunger and nutrition advocacy groups at the local, state, and national level. This small program provides critical seed money for a range of local and state projects to alleviate hunger and restore millions of Americans to food self-sufficiency.

State Children's Health Insurance Program

www.cms.hhs.gov/lowcosthealthinsfamchild/

Originally created in 1997, CHIP is Title XXI of the Social Security Act and is a state and federal partnership that targets uninsured children and pregnant women in families with incomes too high to qualify for most state Medicaid programs but often too low to afford private coverage. Within federal guidelines, each state determines the design of its individual CHIP program, including eligibility parameters, benefit packages, payment levels for coverage, and administrative procedures.

Temporary Assistance for Needy Families

www.acf.hhs.gov/programs/ofa/tanf/about.html

TANF provides assistance and work opportunities to needy families by granting states, territories, and tribes the federal funds and wide flexibility to develop and implement their own welfare programs. The assistance is time-limited and promotes work, responsibility, and self-sufficiency. The TANF block grant is administered by state, territorial, and tribal agencies. Citizens can apply for TANF at the respective agency administering the program in their community. The federal government does not provide TANF assistance directly to individuals or families.

provide services. City or county websites should have links to the various departments that serve the poor. These sites may also have links to non-government agencies that provide services. Again, local governments often provide funds and evaluation while others provide the service.

Using St. Louis as an example, the Department of Human Services (DHS) manages programs but does not provide direct help to clients. The city lists DHS service points within the city limits. The city's Veterans Affairs office coordinates services for city veterans who are at risk because they are poor or have poor living conditions. The city sponsors employment and job training programs and has a directory of services for veterans. DHS administers a summer food program for children, the homeless, and the elderly. This department has a mentoring program as part of the city's juvenile court system, runs a collaborative that supports after-school and summer programs, and funds expansion of high-quality early childhood programs. St. Louis also has a disability advocate, a homeless services division, and an agency on aging.

By way of comparison, in Pueblo County, Colorado, there is a Department of Housing and Human Services that administers housing services and rent assistance and a Department of Social Services that provides welfare services to low-income adults and children. There are also veterans' services in this department, but no obvious services for the homeless. There is a Senior Resource Development Agency that manages programs for the elderly and a city-county Health Department. The city of Pueblo links to county services for the poor. Pueblo County does offer a 2-1-1 service that helps low-income people find the county services they need. It also coordinates volunteers and donations for people who want to help the less fortunate. The county has several offices in towns and the city of Pueblo, but there is a push for people to get information by phone and to apply for benefits online.

Each locale has its own names and organization for services for the poor, so the librarian needs to take the time to get a basic sense of how services are provided and where to get information for those who need or want government help. With the trend for more and more information and regulations/applications accessible online, the library has the opportunity to help the poor use computers to gain access to vital government services.

NONPROFIT PROGRAMS

In most communities, there are organizations that serve the poor but are not administered by any level of government. These organizations may have a specific mission in a specific neighborhood, like a Boys and Girls

Club, or have an array of services offered to anyone in need, such as the Red Cross or the Salvation Army. Most communities have a United Way or other umbrella agency that coordinates donations to several charity or nonprofit organizations. The United Way often facilitates collaborations among service organizations, researches problems within the community, and provides up-to-date information services to help people find the services they need through their 2-1-1 service.

Nonprofit organizations have a board of interested citizens who raise funds and oversee the budget and policy along with volunteers who help provide the services and often at least one staff person who manages the services and the budget. Many nonprofit organizations get financial support from corporations, individuals, foundations, and government grants to provide specific services. To get this support, nonprofit organizations register to become a not-for-profit corporation with a federal 501(c)3 tax status or some similar tax designation to receive and spend funds outside of IRS requirements. Librarians may be able to partner with the community nonprofits to market the library's service, to learn more about available services, and to attract audiences for library programs. Nonprofit organizations can be partners in grants the library may want to obtain in order to support programs for the poor.

Many nonprofits have a national, state, and local presence, and there is a vast array of types of operations and services to find out about.

National/State Programs

There is an impressive array of nonprofit organizations that offer, fund, or support services for the poor. Like government agencies, many national and state organizations develop programs that are carried out at the local level. Many of these agencies are funded in part and work closely with government programs. For instance, the Salvation Army is a mission-based international organization that offers homeless service nationally (among other services). It has temporary shelters, counseling, family services, and soup kitchens run and funded locally. Though it is a religious organization, it serves all people in need. Catholic, Lutheran, Jewish, and other faiths have national networks that provide some services to the whole community.

There are many health-related foundations that fund service for low-income or uninsured people. For example, the Susan G. Komen Foundation raises money to "find a cure" for breast cancer. Much of the money raised supports biomedical research, but in about twenty-five U.S. locations it also supports mobile mammography service for poor women, develops culturally appropriate mammography service for immigrant women, and funds further medical treatment for poor or uninsured women who have breast cancer. Information about these services is available at www.komen.org.

AARP provides a variety of services for anyone over the age of 55. Most services are useful regardless of income, but the organization also funds services for low-income seniors. It has specific study groups for issues related to the elderly poor and funds food discounts and legal services to low-income seniors. Information on these services is available at www.aarp.org.

Another national organization that offers services useful to the poor is the YMCA. As of 2009 there are more the 2,600 local YMCA organizations serving children, families, and individuals. Started as an organization serving Christian men, it now serves both genders, all faiths, and all income levels. Individual Ys offer day-care centers and after-school programs, sport and recreational programs, and support programs for military families. The organization also provides training and opportunities for volunteering and offers financial assistance to people who cannot afford fees for their services. The average Y user earns less than the U.S. median income. To find local Ys, go to www.ymca.org. The YWCA (www.ywca.org) offers some of the same programs as the YMCA but also includes domestic violence and shelter services, economic development programs for women, and leadership training for girls and women. Both Ys offer local programs and engage in national and state advocacy.

Local Nonprofit Programs

Most communities have an array of local nonprofit organizations that serve the poor. Homeless shelters and food pantries are often run locally without national affiliation and often without federal or state funding. Local sports teams often provide programs that benefit low-income people and distressed communities. Local businesses create foundations that fund local programs, and colleges and high schools frequently organize students to raise funds or provide services that help the poor. Individuals organize charities to meet a need that is important to them. Local churches help the poor in their congregations as well as in the neighborhood or larger community.

The librarian's first challenge is to find local charities and understand what they do and who they serve. Even small communities may have twenty churches and other charity organizations as well. Cities and large metropolitan areas have thousands of nonprofit groups. Keeping track of these organizations is a real challenge; leadership changes, funds diminish or increase, and addresses shift. Keeping up with the mission of these organizations and having enough information to refer people in need to local charities accurately are time consuming. Some libraries operate information and referral services or work with city government to keep files or websites up to date. Such work is labor intensive and, if done correctly, is never ending because updates are always necessary.

Libraries should be aware that local groups may be good partners for the library as they serve the poor. These can be service partners—telling stories at a homeless shelter or teaching the unemployed how to apply for a job online in a church basement. The library may have funding partners who provide financing for library outreach to an immigrant population or a card campaign for Head Start families. Nonprofits can help market library service to the poor through displays in health clinics or church newsletters promoting the library's summer reading club. See chapter 13 for more detail about library partnerships.

Librarians may also find it useful to be members of charity boards or participate in United Way study groups as a way to find out what issues are important and how the service needs of the poor, or the poor themselves, are changing. Librarians should also recognize that professional contact with health, employment, and social workers provides a variety of knowledge sources with specific expertise to advise the library on how best to serve those in need. Often these professionals are glad to advise the library informally about developing, marketing, or evaluating programs for the poor, and they may be willing to serve on library committees to help target services to the poor.

Each community has its own combination of services to the poor. Some work well; some don't. Funding and leadership in these organizations change often, so currency of information is a challenge. Not all poor people need the same help, and the best libraries have the information needed to direct each individual or family to the community service provider they need. Further knowledge of the services available enriches the librarian's understanding of the issues and the possibilities for cooperation with other government and nonprofit organizations. It is a way for libraries to become essential both to the poor and to those serving the poor.

IMPORTANCE OF THE LIBRARY'S ELECTRONIC MASTERY

If there is one area of a library's work that must involve staff mastery of the Internet in all of its manifestations, it is work on behalf of the poor; so much of the federal government's work, as well as that of many agencies of state and local governments and not-for-profits, is transacted on the Web (see box 8.2 for examples). To be effective, library information has to be accurate and current. Knowledgeable use of online sources is the only way to locate and check this rapidly changing information. And because the poor may have little access to computers outside the library and have fewer searching skills, they may need more guidance in finding, understanding, and using online information than other users.

Box 8.2
NONPROFIT/GOVERNMENT ORGANIZATIONS SERVING THE POOR

Demographic Information

U.S. Census Bureau (www.census.gov) provides annual estimates by state and some cities of various poor and low-income populations.

Kids Count (www.kidscount.org) provides children and family information that identifies children at risk by states and most cities. This is a project of the Anne E. Casey Foundation.

U.S. Administration on Aging (www.agingstats.gov) provides information on older citizens.

Homelessness

U.S. Interagency Council on Homelessness (www.ich.gov) represents more than twenty federal agencies that provide support for the homeless.

National Coalition for the Homeless (www.nationalhomeless.org) is a nonprofit group that advocates for the homeless and identifies services for the homeless by state and local organization.

Salvation Army: Adult Rehabilitation (www.salvationarmyusa.org) provides shelter and services for the homeless. This site has links to local services.

Hunger

U.S. Department of Agriculture (www.usda.gov) food and nutrition division oversees the SNAP (food stamp) program.

Feeding America (www.feedingamerica.org) is a coalition of food banks that provides a locator for local organizations that collect and distribute food to food pantries and soup kitchens.

Literacy

U.S. Adult Education and Literacy (www.ed.gov/about/offices/list/ovae/pi/AdultEd/index.html) is the federal agency that provides programs for adult learners.

National Center for Family Literacy (www.famlit.org) is a foundation that provides information about family and children's literacy and has links to local programs.

ProLiteracy (www.proliteracy.org) is a foundation that provides literacy programs around the United States. It was formed by the merger of Literacy Volunteers of America and Laubach Literacy.

Immigration

U.S. Citizenship and Immigration Services (www.uscis.gov) is the federal agency that provides citizenship services and applications for green cards, visas, and citizenship.

U.S. Committee for Refugees and Immigrants (www.refugees .org) is a coalition that provides resettlement service for immigrants. There are links to local agencies.

Veterans

U.S. Department of Veterans Affairs (www.va.gov) is the federal agency that offers support to veterans and military families and operates military cemeteries.

Veterans Service Organization Directory (www.vso-usa.com) provides links to many veterans' websites (AMVETS, Veterans of Foreign Wars, etc.).

Ex-Offenders

U.S. Department of Justice, Community Capacity Development Office (www.ojp.usdoj.gov/ccdo/) provides services and employment training for ex-offenders with links to local programs. Also runs the Weed and Seed crime prevention programs in many low-income neighborhoods.

ExOffenderReentry.com is a publisher of information to help ex-offenders get jobs and adjust to life outside prison.

NINE

General Library Programs That Help the Poor

THIS CHAPTER along with chapters 10 and 11 summarize programs that our professional experience and formal evaluations indicate are meeting the needs of poor persons within the core values of the library mission. Most have operated on a sustained basis, usually for many years. This chapter and chapter 10 on public access computers examine general programs designed to move the library toward providing more help to the poor. With a little tweaking, some additional resources, or even just a twist in the method and message in publicity, these programs may result in broad demonstrable assistance to the working and chronically poor. Chapter 11 outlines programs developed specifically for library users who are poor. In many cases, these programs improved the quality of broader library programs as well.

Many of the programs discussed in these three chapters are those we developed at SLPL during our time there. We use these examples because we know how they worked and because we did many assessments of their success with users, including poor users. We also know that these successful programs existed over a long period, usually many years. The other issue that we considered is the centrality of the program for the poor, both to them and to the overall work of the library. It is our observation that a good many programs for the poor have been developed and operated at the periphery rather than the core of the library service mandate. Peripheral programs that are done only once or over a very short period often are more about marketing than about high-quality library service.

ELECTRONIC INFORMATION

Boston Public Library and Chicago Public Library have information on the websites and as handouts about how to use public transportation to get to each library location. These include bus stops and metro/subway stops.

Benefits to the poor. This is a way to make getting to the library easier for those who do not have a car.

SLPL created Electronic City Hall—City Ordinances in cooperation with the Office of the Counselor for the St. Louis Board of Aldermen. The library scanned and mounted on the library website all of the city ordinances passed and approved since 1990. The preparation included making sure that the names of all aldermen and all other nouns were searchable, with the opportunity to download electronically or print.

Benefits to the poor. Involved in a dispute with a neighbor, landlord, or business vendor or client, poor persons, like all other citizens, can download the relevant ordinances at any St. Louis branch library without a fee. Before Electronic City Hall, all persons had to go to City Hall and buy a copy of an ordinance or go to a lawyer or a library with local ordinances in books, usually paying to have it printed. The Electronic City Hall benefits all citizens, including those who are poor, by making it possible to get access to the city's legal documents personally, faster and cheaper.[1]

Another SLPL government information project was development of a Business Licenses Database. In cooperation with the Office of the License Collector of the City of St. Louis, the library scanned all the licenses issued by the license collector's office, with electronic copies of fee schedules, instructions for application procedures, and required documents. Anyone starting a new business or adding a vending machine needs various licenses. A new city license collector decided that the website built and organized by the library should be maintained by the license collector's office, thereby moving it to a city government website.

Benefits to the poor. Because time substitutes for money for those in poverty, persons trying to start businesses save time by coming to the library (or any Internet computer) and downloading copies and requirements of the licenses. New entrepreneurs arrive at the license collector's office with all the filled-out application forms and certified checks they need to obtain their licenses in a single visit instead of the multiple visits previously. In short, this project makes it easier for poor entrepreneurs to start their own businesses.[2]

Hartford (Conn.) Public Library has worked closely with the National Immigration Commission to create a library website segment, The American Place, devoted to welcoming new immigrants to Hartford and helping them find jobs, housing, health care, and eventually citizenship. The American Place is organized to include all the steps needed to thrive as an immigrant, even including links to the immigration office so that newcomers can make appointments for interviews and tests without navigating a separate website or traveling to that office just to make an appointment. Hartford's American Place site is in an open Internet environment, making it possible for staff and library users to have exactly the same information. It is operated by Homa Naficy, who keeps up on all aspects of immigration law and Hartford's immigration developments, thereby keeping the site current.[3]

Benefits to the poor. Newcomers to Hartford find their public library's American Place website an excellent orientation to life in the region, including the socializing involved in ethnic celebrations and advice on how to be successful in this country, including becoming a naturalized citizen. In some cases, the website functions the way old large-city ethnic newspapers did, acting as a helpful advice column with elements of how to become a full citizen in the new country—including advice on how to avoid scams set up by con artists around the immigration process.

OTHER INFORMATION SERVICES

SLPL Government Documents staff obtained specifications and standards for all government contract opportunities, with staff becoming expert on how to meet minority requirements for submission as contractors or subcontractors. As censuses became more electronic in their information compilation and release, SLPL hired a consultant demographer who helped break out local tract data in hard copy (and free-from-copyright form) so that local business people would have easy access to demographic data. The library also invested systematically in processing census updates, keeping local census material as current as possible.

SLPL also established a multiple-computer "Tech Room" adjacent to Central Library's departments of Business and Microfilms, complete with full-time staff coverage so that researchers could get quick help as they searched for business information online.

SLPL transformed our Adult Education department, including regular full-time staff, into a jobs center, with online and paper-based publications on résumé writing, test preparation, GED, and college and trade school opportunities, with financial aid options, so that users could study training opportunities of all kinds.

SLPL held down printing costs so that users could make copies of the electronic jobs-related materials they prepared. We also offered computer use training in basic Microsoft programs of the type used by most employers.

Benefits to the poor. Users credited the library with helping them make job applications and finding jobs, including St. Louis area minority contractors who had bids accepted for jobs as far away as New York City. Many low-income students got financial aid for college and vocational schools because staff helped them use and understand the requirements for aid and how to apply for it.

LIBRARY POLICIES

Enoch Pratt Library in Baltimore gives day passes for the library's computers to customers who do not want a library card or cannot get one because they are homeless. Visitors to Pratt's Main Library and people who forget their library cards find this convenient, but the city's homeless are the largest group of users.

Benefits to the poor. Homeless and poor people find this an easy and effective way to get computer access. All they have to do is ask for a pass— no paperwork, no questions asked.

SLPL worked with its users to set an appropriate fine policy. Some professional librarian advocates suggest that public libraries eliminate all fines and fees on library services to the poor insofar as it is possible to do so. In numerous focus groups and conversations with adult users, many—even most—adults continue to express a preference for low fines and fees rather than no fines or fees. Caregivers often see the library fees and fines as part of their children's education, helping teach responsibility and the value of money to get something you want or do not want to happen. The St. Louis library board decided to keep printing and copying charges to a minimum, so that low-income people could use these services. The library maintained a minimal fines and fees policy but allowed staff extensive discretion to waive fines and fees—after training them as to what our policies were and why we might grant exceptions.

Benefits to the poor. Modest fines meant that almost everyone could afford to pay them. Forgiving fines allowed those who could not afford their fines, or needed to pay them over time, the opportunity to continue to use the library.

PROGRAMS

SLPL emphasized serving children and teens by adding staff to Youth Services and by changing services to accommodate low-income families and caregivers. Among all its expenditures to create essential programs and services, none received more discrete funding (more than $1 out of every $5 of the system's annual income) than Youth Services. Youth Services workers visited 125–150 of the city's licensed day-care centers monthly to deliver classroom collections of books, orient staff to use these books, and read to the children. They also visited as many public and private schoolrooms as school principals would allow with similar programs twice a year—in the fall to point out the opportunities for getting help with homework, and in the spring to encourage participation in summer reading; nearly 30 percent of all city kids participated in the program. Since 85 percent of children in St. Louis are "at risk," this helped underresourced schools and day-care centers have books to use.

Youth Services homework helpers stood ready four afternoons a week and on Saturdays during the school year to help kids with their homework and to otherwise help them engage in fun and creative learning. These staff helped kids individually and in small groups to learn to do specific computer routines, including subject research and gaming. During in-library programs for teens and preteens, the library consistently programmed parallel programs for smaller children in different spaces. Because the older children often had babysitting responsibilities, dual programs were the only way they could attend a program. The library also served lots of snacks.

Benefits to the poor. Because so many of the city's children are poor and so many teachers and caregivers work in schools with few resources, the library tried to get books, children, and adults the things needed to make reading happen. City children's reading test scores improved slightly in association with these programs, although we did not try to measure the statistical extent of library programs and children's reading success. Giving after-school assistance to kids helped the poor succeed as students and helped bridge the digital divide for kids without Internet access at home or school.

SLPL found funding for free appearances of celebrity authors and artists. Any library involved in hiring (or getting donated appearances from) celebrities knows how distinctive each appearance is in terms of audience.

Author David McCullough drew almost all whites and lots of men; Ken Burns attracted nearly the same constituents. Nora Roberts had almost all women of every color; Mary Higgins Clark attracted mostly women across generations, including preteens and teens experiencing their first entry into the "adult mystery genre." "Wee Pals" cartoonist Morrie Turner attracted almost entirely African Americans, including lots of children; African American novelist Toni Morrison's crowd was heavily integrated by both gender and race.

Benefits to the poor. With no entrance fee, every author or artist attracted either folks that staff knew to be poor or newcomers who appeared to be poor. We started and maintained this series of programs in a city with a large poverty constituency because we wanted "to act like an important library" for the people of our city. The operational lesson should be that appearances like these increase the library's visibility as a premier cultural institution in the metropolitan area at the same time that they open opportunities for poor persons to see, hear, and get the autographs of creative persons they would otherwise not likely meet. It is the lesson of "the wider world" writ large for a constituency by a public library.

Charlotte's ImaginOn and Phoenix (Ariz.) Main Library have impressive, heavily used teen areas. Their teen spaces are fitted out with accoutrements to aid in study, formal areas with Internet computer pods where small groups can compute together, multichair study tables, and booths and machines from which to purchase snacks. Board and electronic games are available, and kids are made welcome to hang out, sitting in groups on the floor as well as in the various chairs. There are quiet, semiprivate reading spaces where individual kids can get away from others to read, study, or just sit. Charlotte's ImaginOn includes a media production studio where kids can produce items to mount on the library's sites for Teen Second Life, Facebook, and other online communities.

Benefits to the poor. Kids of every economic circumstance get the opportunity to work with computers, the Internet, and sophisticated media equipment. For poor kids, their library often is the only location where they can compute, create, and get help to develop networking skills.

LIBRARY AS PLACE

"Where should we spend the tax money you give us?" we ask community groups. "In our neighborhoods" is a standard reply. SLPL won two tax elections, heavily supported with critical majorities by the voters of poorer neighborhoods. The use of these dollars went to facilities and service in neighborhood branches. In those campaigns, library spokespersons in speeches and publications made specific promises about improving facilities and collections. The board and the staff kept those promises and communicated keeping those promises in many different venues.

Benefits to the poor. Because of the property interests involved, it generally was easier to expand and rehab libraries in poorer neighborhoods—which were generally in worse condition than those in middle-class neighborhoods. Hence, the library tended to rehab and construct new facilities in poor neighborhoods before those in the middle-class neighborhoods. What many in limited economic circumstance saw was that their neighborhood libraries were receiving top priority, a message they were not used to seeing from city or state agencies.

Greensboro (N.C.) Public Library innovated to bring the new and best to their constituents. Hemphill branch was joined with the Green Hill Center for North Carolina Art to bring together art and literacy, using artwork and activities to inspire and nurture reading. "It takes what the library does and infuses it with art," says Mary Young, who directs ArtQuest, Green Hill's hands-on gallery for children and families. The effort is significant because it is a joint-agency effort to create a new kind of community heritage centered in cultural institutions. "It's the first arts magnet among seven Greensboro Public Library locations and could become a model for libraries nationwide."[4]

Benefits to the poor. "Bragging rights" often are in short supply in poorer neighborhoods. This Greensboro example attracted regional media attention and started a new cultural heritage effort in lower-income neighborhoods.

Many persons with limited economic means live in neighborhoods they recognize as unsafe. The library can be made to be regarded as a neighborhood safe haven. In St. Louis, we faced many neighborhoods dominated by drug traffic, street prostitution, or gang members or gang "wannabes." Our solution was to make library interiors the safest place in these neighborhoods by using open designs and hiring uniformed, off-duty city police officers to help staff the most problematic branches. The police were asked to function as high-visibility library representatives, cooperating with library supervisors. The presence of armed police, including several officers from anti-gang units, had an immediate calming influence.

Benefits to the poor. Disciplinary incidents declined, and neighborhood leaders, elected officials, and kids began talking about public library branches as safe havens and neutral territory. The fact that latchkey-kid, after-school attendance increased served as a demonstration of a deepening relationship between the library and some of its less-well-off constituents, including lots of at-risk kids.

The programs outlined in this chapter were designed as major improvements in an entire library system. Each of them had a demonstrable impact on users from low-income neighborhoods. These users especially were taken by the fact that their library respected them so much that it wanted to bring the best possible benefits of a public library to their neighborhood. A poor African American father, with daughters and wife in tow, on opening day of the wholly new 16,000-square-foot Julia Davis Branch Library, said to us as he prepared to leave the bright, light, new building, "No leftovers for us! We appreciate that!"

Notes
1. The web address for the ordinances is http://previous.slpl.org/cityhall/index.htm.
2. The electronic St. Louis license database is found at http://stlouis.missouri.org/citygov/license/geninf.htm.
3. Homa Naficy, "Centering Essential Immigrant Help on the Library Website: American Place (TAP) at Hartford Public Library," *Public Library Quarterly* 28, no. 2 (2009): 162–175. The American Place is at www.hplct.org/tap/TAP.htm.
4. Dawn Decwikiel-Kane, "It's Art, for Literacy's Sake—The Greensboro Public Library and Green Hill Center for North Carolina Art Join Forces in the Hemphill Branch Library to Serve the Reading Needs of Southern and Southwest Greensboro," *News & Record* (Piedmont Triad, N.C.), November 14, 2004.

TEN

General Services
Public Access Computers
and Their Implications

THIS CHAPTER explores the importance of public access computers (PACs) as learning tools used by poor library users. It shows how different libraries use different service staffing to create different patterns of Internet access. We also speculate on the future of PACs in library settings.

ILLUSTRATING THE DIGITAL DIVIDE

Like everything else connected with poverty, the meaning of the *digital divide* "is both contextual and debatable."[1] The term dates from the mid-1990s, and its meaning has shifted as technology has changed. Today the term is shorthand for the disparities that exist between rich and poor in knowledge about the sophisticated information and entertainment available on networked computers, the ability to use networked computers, and access to high-speed, broadband machines. Those on the wrong side of the divide are effectively cut off from a technology-based route to upward mobility.[2]

A good illustration of the digital divide was reported in a January 2009 *New York Times* story about Tyler Kennedy, a 9-year-old boy assigned to do a school assignment on the platypus. Tyler went to his favorite online reference source, YouTube, because that is where he had learned to go for sophisticated help in playing his Wii games and assistance in "collecting Bakugan Battle Brawlers cards, which are linked to a Japanese anime television series." Tyler said that YouTube is his main reference tool; he follows up with a Google search only for the occasional item that he cannot find on YouTube.[3]

Compare Tyler's worldly experience with YouTube in his home with another 9-year-old without access to an Internet-connected computer at his home, school, or library. To have any opportunity to cross the digital divide and keep up with Tyler Kennedy, the second child needs access to a broadband PAC along with a sense of how to find answers in the electronic information cloud. Without such knowledge and access, a recent Florida study shows, he or his peers will fall further and further behind in technological competency.[4]

WHAT THE POOR WANT FROM LIBRARY COMPUTERS

Beginning in 1994, SLPL undertook an extensive set of focus groups with users. Over ten years, the library and its contractor organized more than a hundred meetings with constituents, asking for their help in the design of new branches and the remodeling of old branches. One message came through over and over: our poorest constituents wanted "rooms full of computers," not so much for themselves as for their children. The adults regarded the computers as an entrance into the educated, literate, good-job world of middle-class families.

This desire was especially seen in poor African Americans and more recently in immigrants who came poor to their new nation. Why, we asked? What did they expect from computers? Their reply in summary was "access to a world of education and better jobs." As one person told us, "When your schools are bad, if kids can use computers at the library, they can educate themselves." It did not matter much how their kids used them; in computing, the kids would socialize and learn to become part of an educated class with opportunities to move up in society socially and economically. Without realizing it, these parents and caregivers wanted their kids to have the kind of educational background that 9-year-old Tyler Kennedy assumed as a given in his life.

One way or another, those who do not own or have access at work or school to broadband-enabled computers know they ought to have them. And when libraries install PACs, the institution's leaders have to do little

besides set them up, publicize their existence, and figure out how to organize their usage to minimize interpersonal conflicts.

People came to use library PACs for all kinds of reasons:

> For kids, the PACs represent an opportunity to catch up with
> their friends (e-mail) and "find out" things they want
> to know about their school assignments (how to do
> homework successfully and faster), the social mores of
> their culture (Facebook), and entrance into the adult world
> (how to get a driver's license).

> Young employed people come to use PACs to look for a
> different job and to do research because their low status at
> work gives them only slow computers without access to
> all websites.

> Seniors come to do their family e-mail and trade pictures of
> their travel for the newest cute shots of the grandkids.

> For immigrants, PACs represent a connection with the former
> homeland and relatives (e-mail, international electronic
> news), with the employment world (job ads), and with
> citizenship (e.g., The American Place at Hartford Public
> Library).

> For the homeless, PACs represent an opportunity to connect
> with friends and family in a social setting in which the
> person can protect as much about himself or herself as
> desired, find shelter, and get information on how to obtain
> free medical care.

> For the job changer or the unemployed person, PACs are an
> opportunity to get help writing a résumé, obtain education
> or training for a new job, or find job listings. Increasingly,
> online communication is the only way that prospective
> employers will accept résumés and applications.

> For the rural person, PACs are an information source about
> other people, employment and living conditions in
> cities, other states, and other nations, a chance to get a
> degree or certification via distance education, a venue in
> which to meet other people with similar interests, and an
> opportunity to learn about and purchase products and ser-
> vices not available in the nearby community.

The list goes on and on. Each person without access to an Internet-
connected computer in the home, school, or office uses the library computer

to construct or fill out her or his social, cultural, and economic universe without being bothered by human intermediaries. In a nation that values privacy, individualism, and upward mobility, people—especially poor people—find free PACs convenient, time saving, and personally helpful.

Consequently, individuals who want library PACs believe that, like books on library shelves, computers should be used for whatever the person wants and needs. They want help when they want it and of a type they believe they need.

Even though the digital divide is "contextual and debatable," the popularity of PACs in libraries is an ongoing testament that the Internet machines represent what Enoch Pratt Library director Carla Hayden calls "leveling" and what we have come to call one of the library's "equity functions."[5] In each case, individuals used their personal time (their most valuable commodity other than their money) to come to the library to use library PACs.[6]

From the first gifts of computers to libraries, the Bill and Melinda Gates Foundation recognized that many individuals needed more than just networked computers. They also needed and wanted instruction in how to use computers and how to use computers in specific ways. That reasoning meant that the Gates Foundation insisted that their donated computers be set up in instructional labs where people could learn how to use computers and the Internet.

LIBRARY RELATIONSHIP BUILDING—OR NOT?

After installing Internet PACs, many library systems found that computer use began to drive library use. In other words, for a whole variety of library users, the desire to use a PAC became the first reason for going to the library—more powerful than checking out a book or talking with a librarian. As PAC numbers and PAC usage increased, many libraries began to plan how to transform computer-use visits into user relationships that had more than one machine-oriented dimension. The difference in attitude toward such activities is exemplified in the way Enoch Pratt Library of Baltimore and SLPL handle requests for help outside of formal classes on computer use.

Enoch Pratt Library

Enoch Pratt Library preaches that, outside of classes, library computer users are on their own, and the Pratt system encourages that independence.[7] Those without library cards, and even those who have library cards but do not want to take time to use them, can get day passes at information desks.

The passes allow scheduling and computer use for that pass holder. The systemwide electronic scheduling system allows users to self-register for computer time slots using the day pass temporary numbers, thus protecting anonymity.

Staff members answer questions, but if and when they are busy with their regular work PAC users are on their own. When PAC help is given, the regular staff provides it—and only in very short, not sustained, bursts. These statements do not imply that Pratt staff do not care; they give assistance if their other research or reference work leaves them an opening. New users attend a class to get started, or have a friend help them, or learn by trial and error. Teens, children, and job seekers get more help; gamers get less.

St. Louis Public Library

In 1993, as the SLPL board of directors was working out its new mission and goals statements, staff already could see that computers were attracting poorer persons, immigrants, and children (especially teens and preteens) to their neighborhood libraries. With additional revenue in hand from a second tax increase in a five-year period, SLPL had sufficient revenue to redo most of its branch facilities, improve material collections, and obtain sufficient space and modernized wiring to connect more computers. Our PAC base was comparable to Enoch Pratt's. By 1997, SLPL had about 300 hundred computers with software and electronic support to connect them to the Internet. By 2002, SLPL had 350 PACs serving a population of 325,000. (As of 2009, Pratt has 550 PACs serving 650,000.)

With at least as many computers on a per-capita basis as Pratt, SLPL created a staff position called "personal technology assistants," or PTAs. These were mostly college students, experienced in computer use, who functioned as over-the-shoulder instructors to people who needed help to accomplish some objective on the library PAC. PTAs also were trained in basic maintenance and upkeep methods to keep the PACs running, thereby freeing library staff to do more professionally oriented work like compiling web links and creating finding aids in their areas of professional expertise.

PTAs became knowledgeable and friendly library staff who broke the ice of initial library visits or first computer use or search routine by helping when asked by PAC users. As they gained library experience, PTAs also became adept in suggesting when it was time for a PAC user to ask for help from a librarian or consult some source other than electronic. That was especially so for kids who had little previous library experience and could not find what they wanted quickly using PACs. The scene in which we live and work is for most of us a hybrid world that requires us to use both electronic and paper-based materials. The PTAs became library relationship builders along with being articulate helpers.

It is easy for any library to be overwhelmed by the flood of users who come to use the library's computers. Implicit in the SLPL PTA helper model is the suggestion that PACs are functioning as a library marketing tool and as a high-visibility, freestanding, library service tool. When people are attracted to the library to use PACs, libraries are faced with a grand opportunity to develop ongoing relationships with them. To articulate the whole relationship, PACs bring poor people to experience the library, and in that experience and those that follow the library can help build user relationships that work to the long-term advantage of citizens as they go about their individual, family, and community life.

PACS, PTAS, TEACHERS, AND CURRICULA: THE FUTURE?

PACs are the most important current tool in equity branch operations, because they attract users who are not attracted by books and reading. PACs generate library visitation if poor persons know about them and know that the library accepts their use of the PACs as a regular part of library visits. (All the rules that Pratt set up to encourage use seem to work, including the ability to use PACs anonymously without having a card.)

Our experience with PACs suggests to us, however, that library leaders need to consider carefully how they proffer PACs in their libraries. We believe that PAC use presents the institution with a learning moment for many of its new library users. Because it is such a moment, users are in the early stages of what could become a long-term relationship with their library and their librarians.

Just setting up the computers and letting people use them seems to us a missed opportunity. New users need help to become skilled enough to use computers successfully. The poor have few other sources of this help and view staff help as a value-added computer experience. The message is "Libraries are places to get help from library staff who will work with you to find exactly what you need, whose staff will save you time, and who can play not one but many important roles in meeting the reading and information needs of you, your family, and your workplace."

In short, in the interest of their users and in their own self-interest, libraries and librarians need to be proactive with PAC users in the same way they are supposed to be proactive with all other types of library users. At what point should appropriate library staff ask a struggling Internet user if help is needed? British commentators already have noted that not providing computer-user assistance is a service negative.[8] The message that libraries and librarians have the opportunity to send to PAC users is this: "We add value to your life. We save you time. And we help you find exactly what you need. When you have more to learn or you want more to read, come see us again."

Staff need training to provide computer instruction for individuals and to have the mindset that it is needed. But this is a natural extension of providing individual reference help, and for the poor it is likely to make computing an option not available elsewhere.

Notes

1. This earlier debate over the importance of Internet computers is covered in Julie Hershberger, "Are the Economically Poor Information Poor? Does the Digital Divide Affect the Homeless and Access to Information?" *Canadian Journal of Library and Information Science* 27, no. 3 (2002–2003): 45–63.

2. Technology consultant Bridges Organization sets out a good current definition of the digital divide: Overview of the Digital Divide, March 22, 2006, www.bridges.org/publications/85. Bridges also offers twelve Real Access/ Real Impact Criteria for ICT (2005), www.bridges.org/Real_Access. Bridges specializes in ICT in developing countries, but note that low-income populations in any nation are affected by the same rules.

3. Miguel Helft, "At First, Funny Videos. Now, a Reference Tool," *New York Times* online edition, January 18, 2009, www.nytimes.com/2009/01/18/ business/media/18ping.html?th&emc=th.

4. Tina N. Hohlfeld et al., "Examining the Digital Divide in K–12 Public Schools: Four-Year Trends for Supporting ICT Literacy in Florida," *Computers and Education* 51, no. 4 (December 2008): 1648–1663.

5. The equity idea received attention from OLOS in a 2004 publication and previously in an OLOS objective, which reads: "Promote equity in funding for adequate library services for poor people in terms of materials, facilities, services, equipment and materials to poor." See Robin Osborne, ed., *From Outreach to Equity: Innovative Models of Library Policy and Practice* (Chicago: American Library Association, Office for Literacy and Outreach Services, 2004). The equity objective is at ALA Policy Manual, Policy 61.1.6 and following, www.ala.org/ala/aboutala/governance/policymanual/ index.cfm.

6. It is good to remember that "going to the library" is not always the first choice of how to accomplish something. Various studies show that, before they go to the library, scholars already have talked with their colleagues and sorted through the materials they keep in their research files; adults have consulted the relatives they like, close friends, and even the yellow pages before going to a library; and most kids want to be nearly anywhere besides in school or at the library doing homework.

7. This chapter has been influenced by discussions with our colleagues Mike Crandall and Karen Fisher at the University of Washington School of Library and Information Science, with whom we have been consulting on

an IMLS-funded research project to ascertain in the most definitive way possible the benefits of public access technology in public libraries. During the course of that research, along with being involved in planning research, report writing, and analysis, we were fortunate to be invited to visit the Enoch Pratt for a week of research and observation of PACs in the Pratt libraries. We, of course, compared this extensive program in Baltimore with our own work and many other observations in this country and others. To Enoch Pratt Library director Carla Hayden and her staff, who shared their thoughts with us over many different days, we express a special thank-you for helping us enrich our concept of an "equity library."

8.   Andrew Brown, "Literacy before Laptops: Technology Alone Cannot Lift People out of Poverty, as the Collapse of a Well-Meaning Computer Scheme Shows," Guardian.co.uk, May 18, 2008, www.guardian.co.uk/commentis free/2008/may/18/chipswitheverything.

ELEVEN

Specific Library Services That Help the Poor

IN THIS chapter we outline a series of library services generated specifically to help poor users. The illustrations show how the library adapts its services to meet the specific needs of different user groups. We also discuss a few special challenges to such projects.

SPECIAL SERVICES FOR SPECIFIC GROUPS

Over time the library's community changes. In that process, those who are poor change, as some rise out of and others fall into poverty. Employment patterns change as businesses start up, close, go bankrupt, add jobs, and lose jobs. To keep up, those who are looking for jobs need different skills. Lisa Payne suggests what those differences mean for libraries:

> To reinvent itself for the future, the library has to reevaluate its role in the community. This reevaluation should pinpoint any discrepancies in service and rectify them, and this often means implementing special programming. . . . Each . . . special population . . . has the right to public library services. . . . Traditional public library services

have failed to meet the needs of these patrons and potential patrons. In order to draw these populations into the
library and provide for their needs, special services must
be offered. Claire K. Lipsman defines special services as
"activities or programs undertaken in addition to, or in
place of, ordinary library services, with the intention of
reaching or serving a disadvantaged population."[1]

In other words, when you set out to create new services for the poor, you
cover familiar ground (library services planning) with a different and very
specific purpose. You assess the need, plan, organize to meet the need, then
deliver the innovative service and evaluate its impact on the need but for
a different specific constituency than you worked for previously.

Here are a group of library services organized specifically for use by
those in poverty.

Computer Training Labs

SLPL was one of the first U.S. public libraries outside the Seattle area to
receive a Gates Foundation grant to establish labs with PACs installed for
access by those on the wrong side of the digital divide. We established these
at our regional branches and at Central, then contracted with staff from area
computer stores to act as instructors until we could train our own staff in
technology instruction. Our choices of databases and applications demonstrated our concern for the whole range of poor families: learning games
for little kids, adult literacy instruction for those with workplace literacy
problems or for GED preparation, Word and Excel for those trying to enter or
hold their jobs in offices, and electronic back files of newspapers and magazines for homework and research project help. As they did in almost every
library, our lab computers and those set into pods throughout the remainder
of most of our locations quickly became so numerous that we had to create
scheduling mechanisms and eventually install scheduling software.

The key to success in serving the poor was formal instruction in computer and software basics and helpful over-the-shoulder assistance as the
users gained sophistication. SLPL created the PTAs to help computer users
individually (see chapter 10). A by-product of the PTAs was that regular
staff also had someone to ask for help, and staff became more knowledgeable and helpful by observing the PTAs in action.

As our colleagues at the University of Washington are proving with
their current research, library computers have had a profound influence in
easing the digital divide.[2] Standing alone, the PACs provide a modern-day
communication tool that can be used at various levels of sophistication
matching both the user's training and what they want to learn.

Library public access technology represents the library at its legatee best, assuming the duties of low-cost or no-cost computer and Internet instructor in a society in which the poor cannot yet afford to own their own computers and in which many schools that serve the poor and many offices and assembly lines that employ the poor do not stress technological literacy as a basic educational component for success in life.

As libraries have assumed public computing instruction and provision, they have responded to the bottom of the educational demand curve, providing basic "how-to" instruction. Other nations furnish a different PAC model that involves training partnerships with private-sector businesses using curricula from companies that provide current and future employees with job entrée and advancement as soon as they complete the library-delivered courses.

BENEFITS TO THE POOR. People without access to computers at home or in their workplace are able to advance their technological literacy to meet job requirements—and they gain access to the world of electronic communication.

Family Literacy Program

Along with a rich program of children's services, SLPL conducted specific activities to help families become more literate. We trained day-care service providers with tools to help younger children get ready for reading and to do reading activities with preschoolers. We qualified to give continuing education credits to workshop attendees by being certified with the state agency that licenses day-care centers. We encouraged day-care providers to offer these same activities to parents and caregivers of the children placed in their institutions. In our storytimes, we trained our program givers to become behavior models for parents and caregivers as they presented. We created Project REAL (Read and Learn) for young low-income, low-literate families that included family reading activities, programs, parties, and field trips.

BENEFITS TO THE POOR. Using the term explored by Khafre Abif, we helped both parents and day-care caregivers become "first teachers" of their kids through family literacy instruction.[3] Both parents and children gained preliteracy and literacy skills from this instruction.

Help Getting Access to Housing by Timely Organization

In April 2008, staff members of Skokie (Ill.) Public Library were able to obtain information about a forthcoming Chicago Housing Authority Section 8 housing lottery. They published the information on their community

website, SkokieNet.org. The item went live on April 11, and "a steady flow
of calls, emails, and visits to the library website" followed.[4]

BENEFITS TO THE POOR. This story shows how a library that is able to
adapt quickly can help a whole group of its users who otherwise would
have to spend their own precious time hunting for the information.

Jobs Center: A Timely Reorganization

Decades ago, Elfreda Chatman wrote in *Reference Quarterly* about the working poor's problems getting better jobs because they lacked the information
they needed. Chatman wrote that "opinion leaders" dominate getting job
leads and training for job skills. Because poor families do not have such
insider information, they need job-searching and career help, which public
libraries can furnish.[5]

In early 2009, librarians at Enoch Pratt Library decided to emphasize
the fact that their library had enormous abilities to help citizens find
jobs. Building on its well-organized collections of jobs materials already
cataloged and arrayed on the shelves of its Main Library business department, Pratt set aside a four-computer complement as its Jobs Center. Users
could reserve two-hour slots to seek jobs and apply for the huge number
of jobs that increasingly were available only online. When demand for
Jobs Center computers grew to be more than they could handle, library
decision makers reserved other computers specifically for job searching
and applications.

BENEFITS TO THE POOR. Throughout the establishment of this innovation, Pratt's publicity emphasized that the Jobs Center was established for
area citizens who needed access to this kind of library help. A spokes-
person for the library also noted that, should more computers be needed,
the library would reserve them for this high use. The additional benefit
was that staff introduced job seekers who came to use the computers to the
other employment-related collections in the business department. Thus,
the library increased the use of traditional jobs materials at the same time
it was meeting the real employment needs of its users.

Equity Branches

The more we became acquainted with SLPL and other public library statistics, the more it became apparent that residents of poor neighborhoods
used public libraries differently than those from wealthier neighborhoods.
After some discussion, the SLPL governing board, as a matter of policy,
designated some branches in the poor neighborhoods as *equity branches*.

The designation was significant because we used different standards for success in the equity branches than in regular branches.

Notably, we stopped worrying about materials circulation as a measure of success in the equity branches, increased community group and agency outreach from these branches, offered more numerous youth services programs, and found funding and partnerships for cultural enrichment programming in drama and music. We did short evaluations at nearly every program, asking users what they had learned during the program. We did more after-school programs so that older kids who were babysitting could attend while the younger ones also attended library programs. Branch success was judged on program attendance and visitation, outreach, and the number and nature of partnerships forged by branch staff.

BENEFITS TO THE POOR. The poor benefited because we matched our expectations and our activities and services to the needs of neighborhood dwellers. In short, we tried to integrate our offerings into their lives.

Youth-Focused Branches

SLPL designated a couple of branches in poorer, kid-dominated neighborhoods as *youth branches.* Collections and services in these branches centered on kids of every age, with "little comfortable corners" where adults could find popular books, read, and compute quietly. We tried to staff these with younger librarians, who might serve as mentor types, and included PTAs and homework helpers, who were mainly college students with free time in the afternoons when kids were out of school without much to do.

BENEFITS TO THE POOR. The neighborhood kids adopted these branches, using them heavily for both study and hanging out.

Family Experiences

In one of several family-related projects, SLPL obtained a grant to pay for buses and organized evening family visits to a children's museum that waived fees to get new users and furnished each parent with materials that helped them teach their kids about science during the visit. As long as there was room on sign-up lists, an adult could accompany many children.

BENEFITS TO THE POOR. In her evaluation of the evening, a mother who brought five children along on one of these forays to a suburban destination wrote, "We couldn't have afforded this visit without you. The library opens so many doors for our family." This kind of experience promotes new use and loyalty to the library.

Performance Venues for Neighborhood Kids

School children and homeschoolers alike often lack performance venues. When kids perform, lots of adults attend. There are new opportunities for families to see and experience the library and what it does. SLPL frequently scheduled student musical groups in branch meeting rooms, on weekends mostly so that parents were not working. One published example: Greensboro Public Library was active in organizing a regionwide African American arts festival featuring local authors.[6] These are new opportunities for families to see and experience the library and what it does.

BENEFITS TO THE POOR. Neighborhood parents got to watch their kids perform "at the library." Appearances were almost always publicized in our regular mailings to users and often noted as well in community communications.

Book Boxes or Book Bags That Help Adults Explain Things to Little Kids

Here are some examples of themed kits from SLPL: "Telling Time," "Zoo Animals," "Learning to Count," and an all-time little kids' favorite, "My Body." Every collection had twelve to fourteen items, including hand puppets, consumable coloring and writing projects, reading materials, and storytelling items.

BENEFITS TO THE POOR. These multiple-item collections were designed to save the time of adult caregivers and create fun learning for the kids— and to make parents and caregivers into successful teachers and guides. For poor families and underresourced schools and day-care centers, this improved the educational resources available for teaching and learning.

Aspirational Programs

"How to Make Your Home Look Nice and Be Comfortable on a Very Tight Budget" was an extraordinarily popular SLPL program. These classes were taught by a person from one of our poor neighborhoods who specialized in helping people do home decoration cheaply. Another popular program was "Personal Grooming for Girls." (Boys, of course, were too cool for this kind of program, although we did find high interest in crafts from boys in our Club Tech activities for tweens and teens.)

In other libraries, we have seen excellent examples of technology programs for these same age groups as meeting both current interests and aspirations. Many students involved with gaming and preparing artistic mash-ups for electronic presentation are thinking about careers in technology. In fact, in many cases in poor neighborhoods, such interests are at least as realistic as "I'm going to be a professional football player, basketball player, or musician" and therefore worth cultivating as part of library programming.

BENEFITS TO THE POOR. With these programs, the library provides much-demanded responses to the specific needs that poor kids see for themselves right now and in the immediate future.

POSSIBILITIES

For libraries that proactively work with a lot of poor persons and families, there are several issues that cause particular stress, especially among staff who tend to hold strong positive or negative opinions about library services for low-income individuals. We briefly discuss two issues here.

Meeting Space Use Policy

Can a homeless group use your meeting room? In a 2003 book, Don Mitchell argues that access to public space is essential to advance the cause of social justice.[7] An advocate for the homeless, Mitchell asserts that the more that agencies privatize and regulate public space, the more we are helping create the "criminalization of the homeless."

A multitude of poor groups want meeting space, especially the kind of safe, clean, and reasonably well-appointed meeting space that public libraries tend to provide. In poor neighborhoods there are few other choices of places to meet, so there may be more demand for the library's space. The "problem" in meeting space use is that when you say a meeting-space-use "yes" to one group, you may be allowing a whole category of groups to use that space. For example, if you allow a popular candidate from a major party to hold a neighborhood rally in your meeting room, must you let any political group hold a meeting there? If you let a community group that publishes a newspaper that homeless men sell on the streets of your city meet in your library, what other groups are you allowing access to the same kind of space? If you allow eight women to play cards in a meeting room on a regular basis, and they start each meeting with a prayer and a contribution to pay for the snacks, have you opened up the possibility of regular church congregations (for those without churches) or regular groups of any kind to come into your cheap or free room and then charge a fee for their meeting?

As one of our friends in the charity business says, "Good deeds always come with a price." Never is this illustration better used than in meeting room policy, especially meeting room policy in poor neighborhoods where there is a shortage of usable and cheap or free community space.

Humanities Programming

One of SLPL's most successful and long-term meeting groups was the Classics Discussion Club we discovered meeting every month or so at one of our branches in a poor neighborhood. The group became visible when a branch manager requested multiple copes of a book of essays by Socrates. Why the need? On a visit to the branch one afternoon, we were introduced to one of the eight members of the club. "I admire your tenacity," I noted. "Yes, we are tenacious," he said. "But the effort's worth it. It's thinking about something else, something important, than what I do for a living." "And what's that?" I said. "I fix cars," the man said. "I love fixing cars. But it gives me lots of time to think. And thinking about life's questions is something my friends and I get from reading and talking about the classics."

Who could resist? The books were ordered—and heavily used.

That group, however, raises the issue about what to do about humanities programming in poor neighborhoods. Several authors have made good cases for humanities programming not only in public libraries but in libraries in poor neighborhoods. One such article, "Digging Deep: The Humanities Approach to Family Literacy" by Cathay O. Reta and Dianne Brady, demonstrates the opportunities those who are poor and caught in ethnic assimilation conflicts can gain from carefully planned library humanities programming.[8]

As Reta and Brady show, really well-planned, well-executed programs in the humanities may do well in poor neighborhoods. The success of these was assisted greatly through the outstanding promotion and by the fact that such promotion was set into a warm and inviting environment already established by a library system. And the topics were of interest to the target audience. And the presenters were lively and could interact with the audience successfully.

On the other hand, there was no worse library program than when we tried to set up a humanities discussion issue forum using university professors funded by the Missouri Committee for the Humanities. We placed the program in one of our regional branches where the staff claimed they had a lot of serious readers. After three programs, with an embarrassing maximum attendance of two persons, we returned the money to the funding agency.

What is to be learned here? Canned programs may not work, but finding a teacher who will spend time talking seriously with neighborhood residents may be the most effective and least troublesome way to go with discussions of the humanities.

We expect readers of this volume to have opinions about other issues that make library work with the poor problematic in particular ways. Our admonition is the same that most realistic library directors would provide: First, get to know your audience before spending time and money on the effort. Second, remember that everything you do with your public, especially with its poor members, has a political dimension.

Notes

1. Lisa S. Payne, "Public Library Support Groups and Users," in *Reinvention of the Public Library for the 21st Century,* ed. William L. Whitesides Sr. (Englewood, Colo.: Libraries Unlimited, 1998), 90–91. Payne's reference is to Claire K. Lipsman, *The Disadvantaged and Library Effectiveness* (Chicago: American Library Association, 1972), 142.
2. Samantha Becker, Michael D. Crandall, and Karen E. Fisher, "Communicating the Impact of Free Access to Computers and the Internet in Public Libraries: A Mixed Methods Approach to Developing Outcome Indicators," *Public Library Quarterly* 28, no. 2 (2009): 109–119.
3. Khafre K. Abif, "At Work in the Children's Room," in *Poor People and Library Services,* ed. Karen M. Venturella, (Jefferson, N.C.: McFarland, 1998), 44–61.
4. Hunger, Homelessness and Poverty Task Force, Social Responsibilities Round Table of the American Library Association, "Skokie Public Library Helps Low-Income People," blog entry posted June 11, 2008, http://hhptf .org/article/400/skokie-public-library-helps-low-income-people.
5. Elfreda A. Chatman, "Opinion Leadership, Poverty, and Information Sharing," *Reference Quarterly* 26, no. 3 (Spring 1987): 341–353.
6. Greensboro Public Library–Hemphill Branch Library on LibraryThing, www.librarything.com/venue/22144/Greensboro-Public-Library ---Hemphill-Branch-Library; Hemphill Library in partnership with Green Hill Center for NC Art/ArtQuest present the Second Annual Cultural Arts Festival, October 8, 2–5 pm, at Hemphill Library, Press Release from www .greensboro-nc.gov/departments/Library/pressreleases/culturefest.htm.
7. Don Mitchell, *The Right to the City: Social Justice and the Fight for Public Space* (New York: Guilford Press, 2003); see also Randall Amster, *Lost in Space: The Criminalization, Globalization, and Urban Ecology of Homelessness* (Austin, Tex.: LFB Scholarly Publishing, 2006).
8. Cathay O. Reta and Dianne Brady, "Digging Deep: The Humanities Approach to Family Literacy," *Public Library Quarterly* 26, nos. 1/2 (2007): 61–73.

Part III
Big Challenges

TWELVE

The Homeless

How Should Our Libraries Help Them?

IN THIS chapter we treat the homeless in the way that libraries generally have treated them: segregated for special attention. Our chapter, however, is somewhat different from most library articles on the homeless in that it is based on survey data in which the homeless speak for themselves and on articles by those who work with the homeless and know the specifics of their conditions. Moreover, it lays out mission-driven services that libraries can and should perform for the homeless.

NUISANCE LAW

No users challenge the librarian's ability to treat every visitor with respect more than those who visibly act out their pathologies. Their dirt, smell, and plastic garbage bags, old luggage, or even shopping carts filled with "their stuff" are the overt conditions they bring with them. Then, too, there are the behavioral issues: no interest in library materials or computers, incoherence of speech, apparent narcolepsy, staring vacantly into space for hours on end or staring at a female staff member while masturbating. If these are not enough to attract staff attention, some visitors manifest symptoms of acute illness—like passing out, incoherence, glazed-over eyes, or depressed or escalated pulse rates—that require staff to drop attempts to deliver library service and instead call for emergency medical service.

The prior paragraph, of course, is *not* about the homeless, but it marks out some of the behaviors prohibited or regulated by nuisance law in our state and many others as well. People who behave as nuisances in public places, including libraries, are subject to penalties like temporary and long-term exclusion from the institution or arrest and prosecution under specific prohibitions or under terms of more general trespass laws.

To sum up, in most states and most locales there are laws and ordinances that deal with aberrant behavior in public places. Libraries, all the persons who work there, and the users who visit these institutions are protected under workplace and public place health and safety laws. Persons with whom librarians have to deal as public nuisances may or may not be homeless, but they are subject to laws just like library workers. As public places, libraries have a right to regulate and deal with public behavior; they do not have a right to discriminate against categories of users.

In working with homeless individuals and families, striking an appropriate balance between the legal duties of a public place and the ideal of free speech for all is difficult at best. If one did not know better, an assessment of library literature sometimes suggests that libraries meet up with no poor persons except the homeless, and that all behavior of the homeless is protected under free speech doctrine. We try in this chapter to overcome some of that imbalance. This chapter contains specifics that we hope help library staff deal with and legitimately serve homeless persons within the context of how they serve other poor persons and their users generally.[1]

ISSUES INVOLVING LIBRARY HOMELESS
Who Are the Homeless?

Let's begin with a definition: a homeless person is someone who has no regular residential address. Advocates for the homeless estimate that at any one time about 1 percent of U.S. residents are homeless, which would make about three million persons homeless every night. Remember that three million number. The other statistics in this chapter, including the percentages, are based on that conservatively estimated total. Unless the person is homeless by choice—and that constitutes roughly 15 percent of those on the street (most of whom are men), their first need is "a place to live with an address." Just for the record, most homeless are not "campers"—sleeping in doorways, in parks, or on stream banks. They sleep in a car or truck, or by permission on somebody's couch or in somebody's basement.

"Our Homeless" and "the Newcomers"

For those who work in a library large or small, there are "our homeless" and "the newcomers." Our homeless are regulars. At particular seasons of the year, on particular days, or at particular hours of certain days, they show up just like our other regulars in genealogy, antiques, current periodicals, or religion and sit by the hour, reading, taking notes, or writing on a sheaf of papers bulky enough to be a manuscript. As with all library regulars, our staff and our homeless users accommodate each other. They communicate regularly; both sides obey the rules. (As one long-term main library professional remarked to us during one of our visits, "We leave them alone. They're using our materials. And they're not hurting anything.")

In some cases, relationships develop. Library staff hold books and sometimes their research notes because they do not want to lose them between library visits. We check out a book to them because we "know implicitly" that it will be returned. We put up with their idiosyncrasies—their tinfoil hats to protect against alien radio waves, their paranoia about people sitting too close to them, even their loud grinding of teeth or their smells. And we offer them help—library help and any information we can find for them that helps them with their lives, whether that be help with their research projects or addresses where they can get a shower or get their prescriptions refilled or see a dentist.

Most of the problems that libraries have with homeless occur because they are "new homeless" who whether rationally or not become loud or obnoxious to other users and to staff. Just like anyone who travels to different cities, homeless newcomers find out that the rules are different from library to library. Our rules: "Yes, you really do put yourself at risk of arrest if you curse out a staff member, or masturbate under the table, or smell so badly that the entire room reeks of your odor." Since odor is such a sensitive issue in libraries, let us point out that in a later section of this chapter we deal with illness and disease among the homeless. A bad odor is one of humans' most sensitive indicators of a health problem; that signal should not be ignored.

What we recommend for working with the "new homeless" is to have staff provide a careful, firm, and friendly approach with ready or printable lists of locations and maps to helping agencies for food, showers, health care, beds, and jobs. That kind of approach falls well within any limiting scope of service statement your governance body may have developed.

What you provide to such persons is an offer of help which, after talking briefly with them, you believe they need. Such an offer shows respect and gives real assistance. It goes well beyond letting someone enter a library room, smelling of their own urine and excrement, watching lice drop out of their hair, and seething because "staff isn't allowed to do anything about that," as one New York City branch librarian told us during our most recent visit.

To make this whole process legitimate and to make it easier for all staff to provide appropriate helpful information, mount all information that will help poor persons, especially those who are homeless, on your public website. As librarian Homa Naficy says about the American Place website for new immigrants at Hartford Public Library, "Staff use the immigration website more than users do. They're always printing something from it and handing it to users as they are talking with them." That is being both realistic and helpful to staff and users alike.

What the Homeless Need First

Because of the shortage of low-cost housing in this nation, getting a place of residence with an address is often a time-consuming and bureaucratic process. In cities where there is subsidized housing for homeless people, qualification often takes time. Like most other help connected with being poor, the homeless have to qualify for housing. If libraries want to help the homeless find housing, they need to know how to qualify and whether or not it is available if they qualify. Most subsidized housing for the homeless fills quickly; there are more homeless wanting subsidized housing than there are units for them.

The most immediate request from most of the homeless is "Where can I get something to eat?" This claim is bolstered by a statistic: 58 percent of the homeless self-report having trouble getting enough food to eat. So librarians need to maintain information on the location of organizations that provide food to the homeless. They also need to make available the addresses of and directions to shelters that offer places to sleep, an opportunity for showers, and places to wash clothes or find out about jobs and job training. And we must not forget literacy tutoring. There is a high incidence of low literacy in the homeless population. Some libraries keep up-to-date printed lists with service, address, and a map showing locations to hand out to those asking, or they simply place them in handout kiosks so that no one has to be embarrassed when asking for help.

If your community happens to be one of those with few or no shelters, no feeding stations, and no nearby clinic or medical center that provides charity medical care, then your staff needs to know that the library administration and governing structure realize that fact. The leaders ought to devise a message so that staff know what an appropriate negative answer is to requests for emergency help. Staff also need to know the issues involved in inappropriate personal volunteering to help that assumes direct or contingent liability for your institution. Usually in small-town situations where no formal helping networks exist, there are informal helping organizations that your emergency services agency staff know about. Silence from library leaders on these matters is not appropriate. Like employees in all service organizations who want to be helpful, libraries have some staff who, when faced with something for which they have no correct answer, make up one.

We also remind libraries of the growing trend to use 2-1-1 numbers as a route to emergency information for anyone who calls. If your region has a 2-1-1 help number, all your staff need to know what is on it and if it works well or badly.

Just like everyone else, the homeless have essential information they want and need that libraries can provide or help them get. Libraries ought to be where they can find helpful information.

Public Access Computers

Librarians need to recognize that access to free PACs has changed the shape of homeless demand for information. When they enter your library, homeless new to your locale often go immediately to PACs to search for information on shelters, health care, and jobs. Many also want to make use of your PAC e-mail capabilities. Some homeless PAC users, like other low-income persons, may need more help finding information they want than they are willing to ask for, and even a little staff help may be appreciated.

THE COMPOSITION OF THE HOMELESS

When you talk or write about the homeless, make sure you recognize that, like the poor generally, they are not one group but many. Here are some of the major statistical characteristics of the homeless.

Military Experience

Twenty-three percent are veterans, compared to 13 percent of the general population. Given our recent woeful history of veterans' health care, these persons, not included in the figures below, may have undiagnosed or untreated illnesses. Also, the difficulty of accessing veterans' medical services often means that they have left where they were trying to get treatment and become homeless.

Health

- 22 percent have serious mental illnesses or are disabled.
- 30 percent have substance abuse problems.
- 3 percent report having HIV/AIDS.

- 26 percent report acute health problems other than HIV/AIDS, such as tuberculosis, pneumonia, or sexually transmitted infections.
- 46 percent report chronic health conditions such as high blood pressure, diabetes, or cancer.
- 55 percent report having no health insurance (compared to 16 percent of the general population).
- 58 percent report having trouble getting enough food to eat.

Another source breaks out medical data using some different descriptors. Relying on "lifetime self-reported . . . problems," this compilation categorizes the following medical and medical-related problems:

- 62 percent alcohol
- 58 percent drugs
- 57 percent mental health
- 27 percent mental health and alcohol or drug (dual diagnosed)

It is this set of conditions more than any other that causes libraries problems in providing services to the homeless. To put the matter precisely, when a staff member or user interacts with a homeless person, there is a fifty-fifty chance that the homeless person is mentally or physically ill. It is that reality that makes Torrey, Esposito, and Geller's *Public Libraries* article "Problems Associated with Mentally Ill Individuals in Public Libraries" so significant.[2] The authors' contention is that, because we have closed the asylums and put the mentally ill on the streets without the commensurate community mental health programs we promised, we have made public library reading rooms into day-care centers for the mentally ill. Based on their estimates, the reality is that ninety-five out of every one hundred mentally ill persons who would have been confined in an asylum in 1955 are on the streets of U.S. cities today.

It was medical realities like these that more than fifteen years ago made the SLPL library administration hire experts from the treatment community to train our staff in handling hostile and aggressive visitors. At about the same time, we began to hire off-duty city police officers to work with our own in-house security employees to keep our staff and our visitors in and around our buildings as safe as possible.

Moreover, we stepped up training in emergency procedures so that every employee would know when to call on-duty police officers and fire department emergency paramedics and ambulance teams. That training included instruction in cleaning up hazardous fluids like blood, excrement, and urine (as well as unidentified white powder; yes, we had to close a branch because of such powder). We also replaced fabric-covered chairs with totally washable covers in many seating areas. Our training and precautions were no more and no less than used by public places like shopping centers, hotels, and schools concerned about the safety and health of their staff and users.

We do not believe libraries ought to apologize for visible security if the user population likely contains pickpockets, pedophiles, or those willing to commit armed assault and theft on other visitors or staff. A strong security presence allows libraries to do their valuable library business with gang members, the mentally ill, and unaccompanied kids, just like they serve the rich and poor, mothers, fathers, caregivers, accompanied kids, and seniors.

Work and Finding Jobs

Jobs are a tough subject for the homeless because a lot of them already have jobs.

- 44 percent report having worked in the past week.
- 13 percent say they have regular jobs.
- 50 percent say they receive less than $300 a month in total income from all sources.

In the homeless who work, we find a new meaning of the term *underemployed.* The job problem of the homeless is that the work they do for pay does not yield enough to provide them with food, clothing, and rent, much less medical insurance.

The easy (and mostly temporary) solution to the jobs issue for the homeless would be for libraries to compile a list of temporary employment services that operate within close proximity to libraries. As with the data on available shelter, food, and medical care, this data should be made available on the library website.

The greater employment problem—for the homeless and the poor generally—is improving their job prospects by training that prepares them for a better job. The question is how involved the library should be in job skill and job search training. At what level of literacy (and technological literacy) should library staff be prepared to provide such instruction.

Education and Low Literacy

Remember that functional literacy problems in some old, large cities like St. Louis are estimated at 40 percent of the population. Education statistics for the homeless suggest the relevance of that estimate:

- 38 percent have less than a high school diploma.
- 34 percent say they have a high school diploma or equivalent (GED).

Many homeless may need help reading applications for housing or bus schedules and help finding books that are of interest but easy to read. Some homeless shelters offer adult literacy programs or GED classes because of the educational deficit associated with being homeless.

Ethnicity, Race, and Homelessness

The "homeless problem" in libraries comes both from our nonhomeless and nonpoor users and from our staff. One of our very good friends who has been a frequent user of our main library for decades told us during one Sunday brunch, "I never go to Central Library any more. It has too many homeless."

The complaint was not about smells or misbehavior, it was about how people look. Sure, it was a form of prejudice. But it was also a kind of defensive behavior that parents in this country have been drilling into their children for many generations (remember: "Stranger Danger!"). In a social setting, like a library, where many people look different from our perception of "us," we tend to become uncomfortable because we are afraid that the situation may get out of control in a way that will embarrass, humiliate, or hurt us. So, our good friend was frightened by what she saw—and what she associated with that visual experience.

Our response was to tell her, "Everyone has the right to use the St. Louis city library. We are sorry that you felt uncomfortable in that setting, but we believe you were quite safe. We take enormous care to ensure your safety and good customer service just like we do for everybody."

Will that make our old friend into a rehabilitated Central Library user? Maybe or maybe not. But we provided her with a shot of education, and we will give her another shot of education the next time we see her.

We make this point in this chapter because the visual sense of difference between homeless and "us" is magnified by the number of minorities who are homeless. Of those who are homeless,

- 49 percent are African American (compared to 11 percent of the general population).
- 13 percent are Hispanic (compared to 10 percent of the general population).
- 2 percent are Native American (compared to 1 percent of the general population).

That is how color (race and ethnicity) gets mixed up in the homeless equation. So does gender. Of the total homeless,

- 41 percent are single males.
- 14 percent are single females.

- 40 percent claim to be part of families with children, which currently is the fastest growing segment of the homeless.
- 5 percent are under 18 years old unaccompanied by an adult. By one estimate, kids are undercounted and their figure is closer to 40 percent of the homeless. The difference between these two estimates has to do with how to count youngsters who are working the streets—in the sex trades, drugs, or other illicit activities—living in "group quarters," communicating by Internet or cell phone, with mail coming to "drops" and post office boxes.

Childhood Abuse and Jail Time

Many of the homeless come out of troubled backgrounds, including time in jail. One survey reports the figures around crime and the homeless in this way. Of the total homeless surveyed,

- 25 percent were physically or sexually abused as children.
- 27 percent were in foster care or similar institutions as children.
- 21 percent were homeless at some point during their childhood.
- 54 percent were incarcerated at some point in their lives.

A different survey reports the following about criminality and homelessness:

> The results [of the survey] revealed a wide range of past and current criminal behavior: as many as 62.4 percent of the subjects had been arrested for illegal behavior, or admitted to earning current illegal income, and 44.3 percent of male respondents had a history of incarceration in jail or prison. Criminal behavior appeared to serve various functions among the homeless, and the homeless who engaged in illegal behavior can be classified as chronic criminals, supplemental criminals, criminals out of necessity, substance abusers, or the mentally ill. While the homeless as a whole engage in relatively high levels of illegal activity, for many this is an adaptive response to dealing with severely limited resources.[3]

In other words, many homeless people feel pushed to crime because they do not have sufficient money to pay for food or housing. Another way of making this point is to suggest that a lack of help for the homeless pushes them to become criminals.

INTEGRATING LIBRARY SERVICES INTO THE LIVES OF THE HOMELESS

What should librarians do about a visitor who smells so bad that others complain? One who acts in a disturbingly dramatic way? One who sits and stares into space or who stares at a certain employee for hours? One who washes himself or his clothes in the men's restroom?

It depends. There is dealing with the rational and with the nonrational. This statement implies that norms exist. And they always do. The question is whether those norms are personal or institutional. A second question is whether or not the staff have training or experience to deal with the matter, whether they try to deal with it without guidance from administration, or whether they run and hide and "let the problem take care of itself."

The reality is that the homeless are poor first. If the library has developed high-quality services and staff training in working with poor constituents, the institution will be able to help and staff will want to help. Job help, finding shelter, meals and health care, and handling emergencies are all services that libraries ought to be good at. And then there are the partnerships and the outreach services, which we discuss in chapter 13. Setting up libraries in homeless shelters, hanging brochures and broadsides in places where the homeless gather, exporting storytime to family shelters where battered women are doing their best for their kids in the midst of family violence—the examples are as varied as the professional imagination.

We conclude with the words of Joshua Jackson, reference librarian at Emerson College:

> While it is incumbent upon libraries and librarians to constantly strive to meet the needs of all of their actual and potential user populations, it is also equally important to develop programs and services that are sensitive to the particular, distinct needs of special user populations such as the homeless. In the final analysis, there is no better test of the profession's dedication to equal and democratic public service than the extent to which the needs of the "least among us" are recognized and fulfilled.[4]

Emerson suggests that the library spirit should be willing to help the homeless. Action will be based on more than exhortation, emotion, or just flat-out stupid behavior if the infrastructure of training and resourcing for service is in place as well.

Notes

1. All of the homeless statistics in this chapter are drawn from the very useful compilation from numerous sources accomplished to complete the current Wikipedia "Homeless in the United States" article, http://en.wikipedia .org/wiki/Homelessness_in_the_United_States#cite_note-SAMHSA-9. This compilation includes numerous citations that can be tracked back to government and advocate-organization reports. Individuals working on homeless issues within their communities, of course, must undertake more specific research. They might want to start by looking over some of the materials reviewed in chapter 8 or just start with the documentation in the Wikipedia compilation. When we researched several of the statistics in the Wikipedia entry, we deemed them satisfactory for the purposes of this chapter.

2. E. Fuller Torrey, Rosanna Esposito, and Jeffrey Geller, "Problems Associated with Mentally Ill Individuals in Public Libraries," *Public Libraries* 48, no. 2 (April 2009).

3. Andrea Solarz, "Examination of Criminal Behavior among the Homeless," paper presented at the Annual Meeting of the American Society of Criminology (San Diego, Calif., November 13–17, 1985), ERIC Document 269713.

4. Joshua Jackson, "Finding a Home in the Library: Services for the Homeless," WebJunction, December 8, 2006, www.webjunction.org/ home/-/articles/content/445200.

THIRTEEN

Partnerships and Collaborations That Enrich Library Services to the Poor

WELL-CONCEPTUALIZED and executed partnerships help extend the library's reach and its ability to serve specific groups in richer ways. This chapter explores the principles of partnership and the management strategies and tactics to make them successful.[1]

WHY PARTNERSHIPS AND COLLABORATIONS

New times call for new tools. In recent decades, library partnerships—the term used throughout this chapter as the name for these various alliances—have grown in number and significance.[2] Four factors have contributed to this increase:

- Networked computers and digitized materials and records have created opportunities for easier cooperation among different government authorities and public libraries.
- Finite resource limits and recent downsizing have created economic pressure on libraries to look for partners to cut costs while improving services.
- The customer-service revolution has accustomed the public to expect all-in-one service at whatever institution they happen to be.

- Citizens and policy makers alike expect their tax-supported public libraries to play an "equity role" in ensuring that society's
  poorer citizens do not suffer from being on the wrong side of the
  digital divide.

For many libraries the downside of partnerships is that they take extra work, and the library gives up some power and autonomy to the partner. Partnerships are difficult to maintain over time as staffs, funding, and missions change. Dealing with different rules of operation and cultures of service may take adjustments by library staff, and decision making can be slowed down by adding the partner's bureaucracy onto the library's administrative structure. Sometimes partnerships are not fun, or equitable, or as productive as the library's own programs. But if done correctly they can expand and improve service to the poor in ways that the library cannot do on its own.

Whether public libraries initiate partnerships or are forced into them, joined self-interest is at the heart of partnership successes. Partnerships are successful when each partner gains more by working with another than by working alone. The partners may gain unequally, but each must be able to measure or to at least sense the gain. Whether formal or informal, all partnerships are relationships that need appropriate planning and sound operating principles if they are to avoid sour endings.

Partnerships take time and often funding to work effectively. Most partnerships demand ongoing attention to keep on track. And, to put the matter simply, some partnerships ought not to happen. The best time to stop bad partnerships is before they are begun, not after they have become an operational mess and a communications nightmare.

TYPES OF PURPOSEFUL PARTNERSHIPS

We categorize library partnerships into seven types. Here are the seven, with examples from SLPL.

Training Partnerships

Focus St. Louis is a community capacity-building organization that has been training community leaders for more than two decades. We asked its trainers to give all our staff practical lessons in community demographics and history. This training made our staff more sophisticated in their customer relations and helped them realize the huge extent of the unserved in our geographic service area. Without substantial training relationships, the library could not have moved forward so quickly to enhance delivery services to our poor constituents. The library got high-quality training, and

Focus St. Louis was able to meet its goal of community building. Because the library staff knew more about the city's poor, they developed better services to serve them.

Funding Partnerships

The basic theme of library funding partnerships is always the same: the institution obtains new resources, and the donor gains association with an effective, high-visibility, public-service organization working to improve the quality of community life. A funding partnership involves a relationship where funder and recipient size up opportunities. Our relationship with Commerce Banks was one such funding partnership. For SLPL, it involved receipt of a tract of land for a new branch, multiple donations for children's programs, donations to underwrite a breakfast lecture on the future economy by a Wall Street commentator, another to underwrite year-round African American programming, and a third to underwrite the full cost of a branch children's computing area. SLPL gained funds, and the bank gained community visibility in inner-city neighborhoods as it opened and rehabbed bank buildings there. Because of funding partnerships, one of the poorest neighborhoods in St. Louis got a new, large and modern branch.

Information Dissemination Partnerships

Along with a partnership with the Board of Aldermen to publish electronically the ordinances of the city (see chapter 9), we partnered with BJC Healthcare and the YMCA to give books and instruction on prereading to new mothers. We also partnered with the International Institute of St. Louis to mount a library exhibit that illustrated new immigrant women changing the subjects of their sewing when they arrived in the United States. We partnered with area high school alumni associations to set up exhibits that helped tell the story of their schools. All of these partnerships led to increased visibility for the library and the partnering agency and vastly improved distribution of information about each. Through these programs, the poor were made aware of library services and programs that would help them. We were able to serve specific, target markets within the poor population.

Service Improvement Partnership

SLPL partnered with Children's Hospital to provide access to medical social workers for library users who were learning how to cope with childhood illness. They suggested materials for purchase by the library and made fliers about services at the library to give to parents of hospitalized children. The FHA provided information on home purchase and mortgage loans through programs and printed material aimed at first-time home buyers. A group of social workers did programs on preventing child abuse and "Hands are NOT for Hitting" storytimes for preschoolers, their parents, and their caregivers. These other professionals reached audiences of mostly poor city people, and the library got high-quality programs and information that we did not have the expertise to provide ourselves.

Partnerships to Build and Share Audiences

The largest and most successful of SLPL partnerships was with the St. Louis Baseball Cardinals. The Cardinals sponsored the summer reading club and gave pairs of tickets to kids who completed the reading program at the library. The specifics of the gifts varied from year to year but always included tickets plus additional premiums. The library won because kids found the association with the Cardinals so appealing. The baseball club won because the number of minorities in the stands increased, and the library made sure that the club got good publicity from the partnership. Poor and low-income people were able to attend a baseball game, and more kids joined the program because of advertising the Cardinals provided.

Research Partnership

There is an enormous need for public libraries to undertake applied research that is vital to their own futures. SLPL has an applied research tradition that extends back many decades.[3] In the past decade this research tradition has become a major effort.

SLPL's partnership with the social science and behavioral science faculties at Southern Illinois University at Edwardsville is based on contract work for hire, a respectable aside for all academic professionals. In each of its research projects, SLPL has raised the funds from a third party or paid for the research out of its own operating expenses. In almost every case, the SLPL funds have been used to hire graduate students working under the supervision of their professors, with some modest per-diem consulting fees to the principal researchers involved. The academics, however, do get to use data from the SLPL studies to further their academic careers—within the limits of national and federal confidentiality laws.

The research partnership began with the study of St. Louis demography, an attempt to describe inter-census population movements in an effort to tailor branch services to distinctive neighborhood cohorts. This demographic research went in two directions. The first involved SLPL staff overlaying census-track population counts on the geography of library checkouts as measured by library system computer transactions. This staff exercise resulted in a significant policy document that allows library management to better tailor services to meet neighborhood population needs. The library staff used demographic research to plan on the basis of accurate information, and we recognized changes in both the young and the immigrant populations in a timely fashion.

The second demographic research direction started when SLPL staff attempted to define cohort movement and characteristics even as the detailed data from the 1990 federal census grew more out of date. The need for current statistics led to estimation, and that led to the principal demographer at Southern Illinois. Before this project ended, it had yielded not only current demographic estimates for the population of the city of St. Louis but also the development of the SLPL Geographic Information System, which as soon as it was developed was offered to the public. When information about this evolution was diffused through the library world, SLPL received recognition as the first public library in the United States to mount such a system for its own work and for the use of researchers from the general public.[4]

Political Partnerships

In 1993 the SLPL board of directors began to discuss the issuance of general revenue bonds to speed the capital improvement of branch facilities. The problem was that the laws of the state of Missouri then allowed large public libraries to issue bonds only for new construction. This specific admonition prohibited SLPL from using its credit to issue bonds so that the people of St. Louis could gain "improved branch libraries before our kids graduate and we die," to use the words of one disgusted library user.

Finding out about this discussion from the public record minutes of the SLPL board, a library user who was a senior public bond counselor at Stifel Nicholas, a stock and bond brokerage company, offered to take up the library's cause. The Stifel offer was to pay all lobbying costs to get the Missouri General Assembly to broaden the terms of the public library bonding law. Stifel Nicholas asked that if the change were successful and the library issued bonds, that company would be given consideration to serve as principal bond counsel for the issue. The board agreed, after ensuring that Stifel Nicholas would provide documentation that the company's issuing fees were competitive. This action was taken in open meeting and publicized through an SLPL press release. An item announcing the action appeared in the region's most prominent business weekly.

The Stifel lobbying effort was successful, with passage of the new bonding law in 1996. In July 1998, under the terms of the new law, SLPL issued $16,500,000 in fifteen-year, insured, AAA-rated, general-revenue bonds with interest rates ranging from as low as 4.55 percent to a high of 5.2 percent. Stifel Nicholas served as principal bond counsel for the sale.

Like most partnerships, this one was based on a joint interest. It was unusual even by U.S. standards, however, in that the private-sector broker and public-sector library shared risk. Stifel assumed a financial outlay to pass the bonding law. SLPL risked a shift in its public image brought on by its first assumption of long-term debt—which institutional leaders did have to explain to the press. It also risked criticism for making an alliance profitable to Stifel, although the conditions to ensure a good deal for the library were carefully defined both by board resolution and by contract.

The real winners from the partnership, however, were the people of St. Louis, who now will have all new and rehabbed library branches in five years rather than over a ten- or fifteen-year period. A poor city got a financial tool that allowed us to get more for our money.

OTHER LIBRARY PARTNERSHIPS WITH PUBLIC AND PRIVATE ORGANIZATIONS

New York State has been involved in a partnership with many other agencies including public libraries to encourage summer reading as a way to improve literacy and student achievement. The work that goes on under this partnership is amply documented in a 2009 New York State Library report.[5] Literacy partnerships, rightfully, are a big business in libraries. PLA and ALSC have developed many documents with policy and practice suggestions in this area.[6]

Rochester and Monroe County (N.Y.) Public Libraries and the Strong National Museum of Play operate a partnership that gains visibility and audience for both parties. Soon after you enter the Strong National Museum of Play, in Rochester, you pass by a library kiosk labeled the Grada Hopeman Gelser Library, which is a branch of the Rochester and Monroe County Public Library. As you walk around this interactive, high-tech museum, you see signs meant for literate children and accompanying adults that provide information on interpretation, explanation of processes, and tips on how to help youngsters learn concepts and facts. In an alcove or along a wall of nearly every exhibit is a set of bookshelves with books for kids of every age, so that kids alone or adults and kids together can learn more about exhibit content. Finally, there are places to sit, ranging from benches to overstuffed couches, where caregivers and kids can read together.

Tulsa (Okla.) Public Library and various community groups established the Tulsa Day Center for the Homeless (www.tulsadaycenter.org) funded by donations from the private sector. The mission of the Day Center is to provide a safe, healthy environment for people who are homeless and to offer them opportunities and encouragement for achieving self-sufficiency. The Day Center is the only daytime shelter in Tulsa for people who are homeless or in need. Services include intensive case management, a free nurses' clinic, shower and restroom facilities, telephones, community voicemail, a clothing room, a mailing address, and a locked storage area.

Chicago Public Library sports a special "partnership" website that holds the logos of a dozen for-profit and not-for-profit organizations that partner with the library:

> The Chicago Public Library (CPL) is a place where people can come together to participate in a wide variety of program opportunities. CPL is at the forefront of joining with cultural and educational partners such as the Chicago Public Schools, Chicago's museums, non-profit organizations, our sister city departments and the private funding community, to create innovative programs such as *One Book, One Chicago, Great Kids Museum Passports, Chicago Matters* and *Teacher in the Library* which have become benchmarks for Library programs across the country. The branch librarians create wonderful programs and partnerships which reflect the information and entertainment needs of their local community.[7]

All these programs give more resources to poor kids who depend on the library for learning, culture, and fun.

BENEFITS TO THE POOR

Every one of the partnerships reviewed above brought substantial benefits to poor families. Training partnerships meant better overall service and specific assistance in working with users who were under emotional stress. Information dissemination partnerships led to increased visibility for the library and the partnering agency and vastly improved distribution of information about the partnered organizations and their members past and present. When library services were expanded through reciprocal lending, residents gained in the number of libraries where they were treated as regular users. That richness helped minority students bussed as part of desegregation programs and those who commuted to work outside their library district. And when partnerships got free tickets to cultural attractions for poor families, they were able to provide experiences that the families could not afford without the library's help. Political alliances and research alliances give libraries access to resources that they could hardly dream of without them.

Of course, partnerships have to be thought through carefully. But there is plenty of help available specifically for libraries from ALA, PLA, and the Urban Library Council, to name only a few of the prominent sources.[8]

Money to plan and give partnerships often is available through IMLS and grants passed through from the federal level by state libraries.[9] A public library can do many things for poor constituents it cannot do by itself by using carefully established partnerships with other public and private agencies.

Notes

1. The framework for this chapter and several of the partnership examples are drawn from Glen E. Holt, *Public Library Partnerships: Mission-Driven Tools for 21st Century Success* (Gütersloh, Germany: Bertelsmann Foundation, International Network of Public Libraries, 1999). Available at www.public-libraries.net/html/x_media/pdf/holt6en.pdf.
2. For more analysis and detail, see the excellent volume by Janet L. Crowther and Barry Trott, *Partnering with Purpose: A Guide to Strategic Partnership Development for Libraries and Other Organizations* (Westport, Conn.: Libraries Unlimited, 2004); see also Tasha Squires, *Library Partnerships: Making Connections between School and Public Libraries* (Medford, N.J.: CyberAge Books, 2009).
3. Glen E. Holt, "Pathways to Tomorrow's Service: The Future of Rural Libraries," *Library Trends* 44. no. 1 (Summer 1995): 188–213; Holt, "On Becoming Essential: An Agenda for Quality in Twenty-First Century Public Libraries," *Library Trends* 44, no. 3 (1996): 545–571; Holt, "Balancing Buildings, Books, Bytes and Bucks: Steps to Secure the Public Library Future in the Internet Age," *Library Trends* 46, no. 1 (Summer 1997): 92–116.
4. Anne Watts, "St. Louis Library's GIS Disseminates Public Information," *Geo Info Systems,* July/August 1993; Watts, "The St. Louis Public Library's Electronic Atlas: Arcview in the Public Library Environment," in *Proceeding of the Thirteenth Annual ESRI User Conference, 1993* (Redlands, Calif.: ESRI, 1993), 2:505–512; Watts, "St. Louis Public Library's Electronic Atlas: A Successful GIS Application in the Public Library Environment," in *Geographic Information Systems and Libraries: Patrons, Maps, and Spatial Information,* Graduate School of Library and Information Science, 32nd Clinic on Library Applications of Data Processing, 1995, University of Illinois at Urbana-Champaign (Urbana-Champaign, 1996), 213–219.
5. New York State Library, 2009 New York Statewide Summer Reading Program: Research/Promoting Literacy, www.nysl.nysed.gov/libdev/summer/research.htm.
6. PLA and ALSC, Partnerships (2007), www.ala.org/ala/mgrps/divs/alsc/ecrr/resourcesab/parnerships/partnerships.cfm.
7. Chicago Public Library's programs and partnerships page: www.chipublib.org/eventsprog/programs/index.php.
8. See, for example, Urban Libraries Council, *Leading the Way: Partnering for Success,* Urban Staff Development Series (Evanston, Ill.: Urban Libraries Council, 1997). For material ordering, the ISBN is 1-885251-16-5.
9. See, for example, *CLENExchange* 22, no. 4 (June 2006), www.ala.org/ala/mgrps/rts/clenert/newsletter/june2006clenex.pdf.

FOURTEEN

Evaluating Library Services to the Poor

PART OF ANY good plan for serving the poor is evaluating how well the library has done in implementing activities, services, and programs to help them. What evaluation needs to be done as well as the mechanics of who will do it, how information will be gathered, and timing should be decided as part of the strategic plan for delivering services to the poor. Librarians should figure out how they will know they have been successful as well as how they will identify things that need to be done better. Often modest adjustments can increase the impact of an activity and sometimes can reduce the costs of dollars and staff time.

WHY EVALUATION

Librarians are well suited to evaluation. They are trained to be critical: Which is the best book on job searching? What website is the easiest to navigate? Which library programs are important to offer? Libraries are data driven: they collect a lot of information about transactions both electronically (circulation, cardholding, and visitation) and by hand (reference, program attendance), and they have databases of this information that we can mine. And yet library evaluation tends to be, at best, the professions' stepchild—acknowledged but not really part of the family. Or, at worst, it is the five-hundred-pound gorilla in our midst that we try hard to control by feeding occasionally and ignoring as much as we can.

It is especially important to overcome our reservations and build on our strengths in measurement to implement systematic evaluation of services to the poor. As with many target audience groups, it can be difficult to identify the poor who use libraries informally, let alone to understand the effects of the library on the poor. As discussed earlier in this book, identifying the poor, developing services that are both practical to provide and valued by the users, and drawing the poor to the library can be complex.

Evaluation is a tool to help library decision makers as they navigate these complexities to provide high-quality services for the poor. As Steve Hiller and James Self state, "The wise use of data, information and knowledge in planning, decision-making and management can improve library performance. While libraries have long collected data . . . it is only recently that they have begun to use it effectively in library management."[1]

The first step in evaluating services to the poor is selecting the right evaluation techniques and committing to a reasonable schedule of evaluation. The techniques used should be valid—that is, they actually measure the activity of interest. (Does counting the number of children at a storytime at a Head Start center tell you whether this activity helps them be ready for school?) The evaluation should be reliable, consistently giving accurate data on the activity studied. (Do written questionnaires produce clear answers from people who are not good readers?) The evaluation technique chosen should be practical. (Are staff skilled enough to do the evaluation? Do they have enough time to do it accurately? Who is in charge of making sure the evaluation is done correctly?)

Many evaluation plans can be made more doable by using data that the library already collects, sampling, and beginning with simple measurements to build staff skills and interest. A description of evaluation techniques follows.

QUANTITATIVE TECHNIQUES

Quantitative evaluation involves counting something with a purpose. Public library output measures have been used to standardize what is counted and how to put data in context so the information is comparable to other libraries. Most library automation systems "do the math" in that the counts for circulation, cardholding, and items in the collection are done automatically, and librarians can program the system to report results on a regular basis in a useful format. Many libraries also have a security gate that counts the number of visitors to the library. Most libraries require staff to count the number of people attending programs and to note the number and type of reference questions answered.

These general statistics might not tell much about how the poor use the library, but they can be enhanced to give library staff useful information about how or if the poor use the library. If a library has identified a community, neighborhood, or zip code where the U.S. census indicates many residents are poor or low income, the library's automation system could be used to find out how many cardholders from this area the library has by doing a sort of cardholders by address or zip code. By comparing this to the total population of this geographic area the library can find out the cardholding per capita in this low-income area. If this number is lower than the per-capita cardholders for the whole population, it suggests that the library needs to figure out ways to attract more low-income users.

For example, a library identifies two zip codes where 75 percent of the residents are low income and finds that the cardholding per capita is 25 percent. The per-capita cardholding for the whole community served is 58 percent. This suggests that the library is not serving poor and low-income people at the same rate it serves more affluent people. These numbers do not tell the librarians why this is true, just that they need to look further to find out what causes low-income people to be far less likely to get a library card.

Since low-income people may use the library but not want to get a library card, the library may have to figure out other ways to get a count or at least an estimate of how many poor people use the library. Since most libraries would not ask about a user's income even for planning purposes and most users would not share that information with the library, the library needs to find a less direct source of information. Some libraries have staff or volunteers ask users as they enter the library for their residential zip code. This can be done once or twice a year. By using U.S. census information to match zip codes to income levels, the library can get an idea of how many low-income people use the library. Obviously for most communities this is an estimate. People may not want to give their zip code, and not everyone in a given zip is at the same income level, but this procedure does use numbers to estimate actual use.

Other libraries give guest privileges for computer use and other services to people who do not want a library card. Some libraries let residents of homeless shelters get some kind of library card. In these cases the library might note a zip code and use this to figure out how many poor people use this service.

Another count that might be helpful is the number of people served in programs or partnerships designed for low-income people. Homeless shelters, Head Start, and low-income housing groups have already screened their users, so only low-income people will be in the audience for library programs or during visits to the library. Keeping track of this kind of attendance also gives an idea of the number of poor people using the library.

Quantitative data are collected and used for evaluation when goals call for increased library use by the poor. A program for low-income elders may have as a goal to increase cardholding by this group by 50 percent. A reasonable evaluation would be to sort cardholders by address or zip code and by age to identify the baseline or beginning number of low-income elderly cardholders. After the library has marketed library cards to residents in rent-controlled Medicaid facilities, staff can measure the increase in older, low-income people who have library cards. Or card applications for the target audience can be coded, and when the application is processed staff can keep a count of new cardholders. Both are examples of quantitative evaluation. We set a goal, we count; we compare the counts to the goal and record the progress we have made in monthly and annual reports.

QUALITATIVE TECHNIQUES

Qualitative evaluation involves finding out if the library's activities were useful or well received by the user or, in some cases, by the community or funder. The idea is that, in addition to knowing how much a service is used or how many people attended a particular library program, it is helpful and important to find out if the users benefited from their use of the library. Qualitative evaluation involves getting information directly from the user or user surrogate (parents of young children, social workers at a homeless shelter, etc.) through written surveys, interviews, or focus groups. Many libraries also use phone, mail, or electronic surveys to inquire about the library's value to the community at large by asking questions of both users and nonusers. The results of such assessments give an overview of the perceived value of the library.

Such questions as "Did you enjoy the program on knitting for beginners at the library?" or "What did you learn about home loans?" at the library program for first-time home buyers are examples of qualitative evaluation. Results such as "75 percent enjoyed our knitting program" or "35 percent of those attending our home owners 101 series could identify three things they learned" help librarians understand user satisfaction as well as the number of people who found the program interesting enough to attend. A library might take part in a phone survey in which citizens are asked why they do or do not use the library. The library might learn more about what attracts users as well as what the impediments to library use are.

Libraries have used opinion surveys and program evaluations to understand user satisfaction better for a long time. Using these techniques in a systematic way as part of a strategic plan is more recent. Outcome evaluation provides a structure to use qualitative evaluation to measure progress toward goals by gathering information on the impact of the library on its users. A library outcome is a benefit that occurs to a participant that results from using the library. When the benefits to many individuals are viewed together, they show the program's effect. In outcome-based evaluation, an outcome always focuses on what the participants say, think, know, or feel, not on the mechanics of the program.[2]

The federal government began requiring any agency that receives federal funds to use outcome measures in some form in 1993. United Way began expecting outcome evaluation from agencies it funds in 2003. Many states and cities use outcomes to evaluate the impact of use of public funds.

So what is outcome evaluation, and how can libraries use it to evaluate their impact on the poor? In outcome-based planning the library describes what benefits the poor who use the library will get. This can be for library use in general, but it is more often used to describe benefits from a particular service or program. The benefits are stated in terms of what the users experience, not what the library does or attains:[3]

Attitude. What someone feels or thinks about something; for example, to like, to be satisfied, to value.

Skill. What someone can do; for example, log on to a computer, format a word-processed document, read.

Knowledge. What someone knows; for example, the symptoms of diabetes, the state capitals, how to use a dictionary.

Behavior. How someone acts; for example, listens to others in a group, reads to children, votes.

Status. Someone's social or professional condition; for example, registered voter, high school graduate, employed.

Life condition. Someone's physical condition; for example, nonsmoker, overweight, cancer free.

Note that all of these are active, observable behaviors or characteristics.

A goal for the library might be that one thousand Head Start students attend library storytimes during the year. An outcome goal would be that one thousand Head Start students say they enjoy listening to stories at library programs.

Outcome statements also include how activities are to be measured (indicators) and some numerical goal of achievement. For example, the measure of Head Start enjoyment might be whether teachers report that children want to be read to after a visit to the library. A goal might be that 50 percent of Head Start children ask to be read to after attending a library storytime (see table 14.1 for another outcome example).

The idea behind outcome evaluation and other qualitative techniques is that it is important to understand the user experience when considering the

Table 14.1
OUTCOME PLANNING EXAMPLE

Model Elements and Structure	Definitions	Examples
Outcome	Intended impact	Homeless men will have basic Internet skills
Indicator	Observable and measurable behaviors and condition	The number and percentage of participating homeless men who can bring up an Internet search engine, enter a topic in the search function, and bring up one example of the information being sought within 15 minutes
Data source	Sources of information about conditions being measured	Searching exercise, trainer observation
Applied to	The specific group within an audience to be measured (all or a subset)	Men brought to the library for computer instruction from the Salvation Army homeless shelter
Data interval	When data will be collected	At end of workshop
Target (Goal)	The amount of impact desired	85 percent of approximately 125 participants

Source: Adapted from Institute for Museum and Library Services, Grant Applicants, Outcome Based Evaluation, Frequently Asked Questions, www.imls.gov/applicants/faqs.shtm.

success or failure of the library or an individual library program. Librarians are good judges of how programs and services work, who uses them, and to some extent how well they are received, but real accountability comes from finding out how users feel about the experiences they have at the library. The library can no longer claim that users learn, enjoy, or change unless they get that information from the users themselves.

If no one at your library is comfortable manipulating the library database or constructing surveys, get help to get started. Many state libraries or library consortia have consultants that might help set up an evaluation program. Some library automation vendors run training sessions or have a customer service person that could help you use your automation system for evaluation. A local university may have a survey service you can make use of at a low cost. The following sources can help with the mechanics of evaluation:

Dresang, Eliza T., Melissa Gross, and Leslie Edmonds Holt. *Dynamic Youth Services through Outcome-Based Planning and Evaluation.* Chicago: American Library Association, 2006.

Durrance, Joan, and Karen Fisher. *How Libraries and Librarians Help People: A Guide to Developing User-Centered Outcomes.* Chicago: American Library Association, 2005.

Elliott, Donald S., et al. *Measuring Your Library's Value: How to Do a Cost-Benefit Analysis for Your Public Library.* Chicago: American Library Association. 2007.

Mathews, Joseph R. *The Evaluation and Measurements of Library Services.* Westport, Conn.: Libraries Unlimited, 2007.

Nelson, Sandra. *Implementing for Results: Your Strategic Plan in Action.* Chicago: American Library Association, 2009.

Rubin, Rhea Joyce. *Demonstrating Results: Using Outcome Measurement in Your Library.* Chicago: American Library Association, 2006.

WebJunction (www.webjunction.org) has several course offerings on evaluation and measurement.

HOW TO USE RESULTS

Good evaluation is evaluation that is actually used. It is used to confirm that the library is actually affecting the lives of the poor, or that the library can make changes to its service to have better effects on users. It does no good to collect data, glance at the results, and never really digest what the evaluation means for library service. Some library staff have a report card mentality about evaluation—that the purpose of evaluation is to judge the staff and to grade how they do. Although evaluation can reflect on individual staff members, its purpose is to focus on what is accomplished, what could be done better, and how to set reasonable goals.

To make evaluation effective, someone needs to be responsible for ensuring that data are collected in a complete and timely way and then tallied and shared with appropriate staff. If the library has a short survey at the end of a program for low-income families, then the answers should be tallied within a few days of the program and some basic analysis done to figure out what the results are and what they mean. If fifty people attended the program and only ten responded to the evaluation, some follow-up should be done to find out why.

At reasonable intervals individual program evaluations should be merged and analyzed. When the program organizer sees results, a few questions should be standard to ask:

- Were responses what I anticipated? If the expected answers were "blue," "red," or "green" and folks responded "square" or "circle," you need to rewrite the questions.
- What do the responses mean? What was right about the program, what did not work?
- What can I change about the program (marketing, content, delivery) to improve it for the audience?
- Is the program worth doing again?

If a service or the library in general is evaluated, give careful attention to who actually answers the evaluation questions. If you want to know about how your services to the poor are helpful, be sure that those answering either are likely poor or work directly with the poor. If you want to know how the larger community feels about the homeless who use the library, ask this group, but also be sure you get information from the homeless themselves. When using evaluation results, be clear about whose input was collected.

Once analysis has been completed, be sure that staff have a chance to see and think about the results. After amending programs and services, plan to continue to evaluate them on a regular basis. Not all programs need to be evaluated at every meeting. Among other things, you collect a lot of data that needs to be managed, and participants may get tired of the surveys. Some libraries sample users once a quarter or annually. Be prepared to report a summary of user responses to the board or the public, and encourage thoughtful discussion about what the results mean.

Gone are the days when the library can assert that it is actually serving the poor and that the services it offers help the poor without data to back these statements up. To assure that the poor are being served in a way that is valuable to them, to the people who work with them, and to the community as a whole, the library needs to provide systematic, ongoing evaluation to back up the assertions it makes.

A little evaluation will help; a little more evaluation will increase the impact of the library on the poor and provide ways for the library to assert that it is essential to the poor and to the community.

Notes

1. Steve Hiller and James Self, "From Measurement to Management: Using Data Wisely for Planning and Decision-Making," *Library Trends* 53, no. 1 (2004): 129.
2. From Institute for Museum and Library Services, Grant Applicants, Outcome Based Evaluation, Frequently Asked Questions, www.imls.gov/ applicants/faqs.shtm.
3. Adapted from ibid.

FIFTEEN

Poverty and Library Essentiality

IN EARLIER chapters of this book we explore many aspects of improving practitioners' ability to deliver and integrate library services into the lives of the poor. In this chapter we summarize some of the ongoing institutional problems that come with implementing those services. We regard these as "big challenges" that have to be faced before the profession can unite to organize necessary services for the temporary and chronically poor.

INCREASE LIBRARIANS' PROFESSIONAL ATTENTION TO SERVICES FOR POOR PERSONS

The U.S. library establishment's first big challenge is the need to increase professional attention to the temporary and chronically poor. Obviously, this book is one effort in that direction. In the 2008 edition of *Managing Children's Services in the Public Library*, Adele Fasick and Leslie Holt write:

> A librarian makes important decisions almost every day and often has little time to consider the long-term impact of these decisions. Yet unless the decisions are based on

a coherent philosophy of service, they may not fulfill the library's mandate. It is through professional associations, literature and activities that librarians develop their attitude toward and judgment of library services. The thoughtful analysis of ideas and trends is the foundation upon which meaningful library service rests. Every professional librarian should try to become a participant in the professional dialogue through which library service can grow to meet the needs of all children.[1]

Change "children" in the final sentence to "poor," and the quotation has even greater relevance for this book.

As Fasick and Holt suggest, in every profession there must be connections among theory, policy, and practice. In recent years, there have been episodic attempts to make these connections. Three recent monographic exemplars, a Canadian applied research study, and an "action guide" stand out:

Dresang, Eliza T., Melissa Gross, and Leslie Edmonds Holt, *Dynamic Youth Services through Outcome-Based Planning and Evaluation* (Chicago: American Library Association, 2006), makes an intriguing and academically sound subject out of how kids, especially tweens and teens from poor neighborhoods, use computers in libraries.

Jerrard, Jane, *Crisis in Employment: A Librarian's Guide to Helping Job Seekers* (Chicago: American Library Association, 2009), is a slim volume with a high degree of practitioner usefulness. Ah, if only every library guide on every subject was this thoughtful, concise, and useful.

McClure, Charles R., and Paul T. Jaeger, *Public Libraries and Internet Service Roles Measuring and Maximizing Internet Services* (Chicago: American Library Association, 2008), is a fine summary and current analysis of library PACs that is filled with useful statistics and interpretative insights, with special emphasis on how needy populations are using the devices.

McCook, Kathleen de la Peña, *A Place at the Table: Participating in Community Building* (Chicago: American Library Association, 2000). This monograph, with roots dating back to settlement house pioneers such as Jane Addams, involves a "community-based" approach to poverty using available community assets, finding revenue, and raising the entire community through planning and self-help. Now a decade old, this book still has relevance for practitioners, as is apparent in the next listing.

Singh, Sandra, for the Working Together Project, *Community-Led Libraries Toolkit: Starting Us All Down the Path toward Developing Inclusive Public Libraries* (Vancouver, B.C.: Vancouver Public Library, 2008). Canadian librarians have traveled a road to inclusion similar to those taken by McCook, community organizers such as Saul Alinsky, and intellectuals such as Michael Harrington. Starting in 2004 under the leadership of the Vancouver Public Library, many Canadian libraries began to cooperate in a project called "Working Together," with the tagline of "Supporting the Inclusive Public Library." The project's 2008 publication is a rich source of ideas about model professional behavior for U.S. librarians. Available electronically, it is especially valuable as an illustration of librarians from many communities working in concert to shape library services to achieve national purpose. We urge caution here, however, because the Canadian "inclusion program" has far different social and economic realities in which to work than those found in the United States.[2]

The central theme of the anti-poverty effort articulated by McCook and the Canadian study is not to provide "more money, services, or other material benefits to the poor." Rather, "the central theme is to obliterate feelings of dependency and to replace them with attitudes of self-reliance, self confidence, and responsibility."[3] This is because during the decades-long, economic bubble our nation has just experienced, "inclusion of excluded groups" replaced "helping the poor" as a major theme of North American library intellectual inquiry.

This reality, like nearly all national movements, spilled over into ALA, specifically into OLOS. Guided by the mandates of its associated member committees and work groups, OLOS has attended to library services for identifiable professional and social (not economically based) groups who have faced social exclusion. This emphasis is revealed by OLOS publication of "toolkits" on new U.S. residents, gamers, mobile services, non-English speakers, older adults, rural and small libraries, and tribal libraries.[4] No doubt, some of these groups are disproportionately poor, but the prevailing intellectual and economic assumption of this approach is that, if libraries behave inclusively toward such groups, library professionals will have done what libraries ought to do. The alleviation of poverty, if considered as part of the advocacy package, is assumed as a secondary benefit of the remediation of social exclusion. We, on the other hand, believe that in such a capitalist society as the United States you have to start with economics to make social inclusion more than symbolic.

These studies and our own small book suggest the amount of ferment that bubbles around the issue of service to poverty groups in libraries and in ALA.

LIBRARY SERVICE ISSUES OF A POVERTY POPULATION

Another issue is the episodic but ongoing discussion about defining the poor as a legitimate service group. To those who say we should be blind to indicators of poverty, we say, "Why ignore observations that will help provide better library service?"

The idea of "serving all the people as if they are just the same" is like the absurd knee-jerk claim that "libraries have something for everyone." Neither mindset is built on the fiscal or operational realities of public libraries large or small. Both ideas give away the human power of analysis and synthesis—of discernment through observation, identification, and judgment about the nature of other persons and the way they behave in different settings. Such discernment is the basis of successful social, cultural, and economic transactions—and often the beginning of scholarly and practitioner insight and organizational improvement.

Such observation has taken on more importance since the beginning of the vast economic mess in which we currently find ourselves. "Invisible poverty" is on the increase. So, too, is poverty from individual illness, loss of jobs, and movement of industries out of the country. Homelessness is increasing, most notably first-time homelessness for people over 50 years old, of whom 75 percent became homeless for the first time after turning 40.[5]

Libraries and librarians need to become acute observers of and preeminent actors in helping pull our nation out of this quagmire. We will have to be tough and proactive to innovate in this way, because we know that public agency revenue always lags behind general economic ups and downs. We can count on more cutbacks, closings, and firings in our professional community in 2010 and probably into 2011 before taxation revenues increase once again—if the economy rights itself as economists generally are saying it will. "Wait'll next year" is the mantra of the professional procrastinator. In reality, now is always the best time to plan and undertake needed change.

STAFF TRAINING

Our next big challenge as a profession is our overconcern about public library marketing compared with our relatively minor concern about service quality, especially service to at-risk populations. Michael Daehn, whose primary business is marketing churches, which are societal connecting institutions like libraries, writes, "Marketing may get people to walk in your door, but keeping them from walking out the door is dependent upon meeting their needs and building relationships."[6]

Nothing could be truer for how libraries integrate library services into the lives of the poor. Daehn, who has consulted for both Disney and Nordstrom, says the biggest problem in church marketing is the people who work there. When they are asked to do a strategic analysis of their church, "either the participants are naïve and over positive or pessimistic and negative."[7] This comment reminds us of one of our profession's most negative but true stereotypes, the passive-aggressive staff member whose professional response is always to find a way to do nothing that brings any changes to that person's work life.

Daehn states that the essence of high-quality improvement in businesses of all kinds is to get all the persons who represent the business into service and message "alignment," that is, to get them all on the same page so they present a unified image and singular practice in their service behavior. In that alignment in your library, do not forget the security, custodial, and maintenance staff, all of whom have considerable contact with many of your economically poor users.[8]

The main way to improve library quality, especially in a library in which there is not much staff turnover, is to train, train, and then train again. It is to supervise work and to hold staff accountable. It is to build teams and team responsibility for work to be done. It is to reward managers who worry about defining jobs that allow creative work and balance tasks that must be done with those that are in many cases satisfying and even fun to do.

When Carla Hayden told us that many of her Enoch Pratt Library staff worked with missionary zeal to help those who came from lesser circumstances in society, she in fact reported both good staff selection and good training and supervision. In libraries, missionary zeal is just as often a function of training as it is a function of personal moral commitment. And a well-trained staff member is far less likely to burn out than one operating at the pitch of high moral fervor.

MEASUREMENT

There are lots of good places to begin improving library service quality—in services for the poor and in library services generally. Most of these begin with statistics. One such source is Sara Laughlin and Ray Wilson's *Quality Library*, which is the newest volume in a series on the application of "the continuous improvement approach" to libraries.[9] Joe Matthews's *Evaluation and Measurement of Library Services* is a great overview place to start as well.[10] One element of the Matthews book is an illustration of how much more measurement oriented public libraries in Europe and Australasia have been than those in the United States. Library measurement is an especially big challenge because so many MLS graduates turned their backs on learning about it when they had the opportunity to add it to their professional knowledge portfolios. Public librarianship is in great need of more statistical literacy and less quantitative innumeracy.

LIBRARIANS AS EDUCATORS

A completely different kind of focus is found in Edmund A. Rossman's *Castles against Ignorance.*[11] In their library use, the poor want the same sense of professionalism and caring that we hope libraries provide to other persons as well. They want friendly, knowledgeable service that offers the accurate help they need. And they want the sense that their trip to the library or their use of a library website saved them time or was such a good use of their time as to make it seem a valuable investment. Rossman's highly personal volume is about the human and humane side of library education—and how to make it both fun and meaningful.

The problem with librarians as educators is how often they try to assume new educational roles without appropriate training in necessary skill sets. How, for example, can children's librarians help kids learn to read if they know little or nothing of age-appropriate learning behavior? How do those of us who respect knowledge and the sophistication it provides do more than shake our heads at the reference librarian who believes that reference is method rather than content, not both?

EMPLOY AGENTS TO TELL THE LIBRARY'S SERVICE AND SUCCESS STORIES

Gwendolyn Mink and Alice O'Connor did yeoman work in compiling *Poverty in the United States: An Encyclopedia of History, Politics and*

Policy.[12] More than 840 pages of text in two volumes, with articles written almost entirely by academics from universities across the United States, this is a superb reference book involving the history of volunteerism, that area of our culture that took Tocqueville's breath away when he observed its complexity and magnitude in charity and politics more than a century and a half ago.

In Mink and O'Connor's wonderful reference volume, there is one striking fact for library professionals. In the five-page table of contents and the fifty-plus-page comprehensive subject and name index, there is not a single subject or name reference to libraries or librarians.

A year or so ago as we thought about starting the writing of this book, we undertook a survey to find out what potential partner organizations working with poor persons had to say about libraries. What could we find out about the work libraries were doing for the poor nationally or locally when we looked at the websites of such organizations as the United Way, YMCA, Salvation Army, and Girls, Inc., and local and state government websites.

Our results were negligible. From our own experience, we know the importance of having "agents" who push our message with constituents whom we frequently have not yet served. Agents are those who not only think highly of us but advocate our use with those who currently are not users.

In poor communities, libraries need all kinds of agents. They need teachers, caregivers, ministers and other faith-based representatives, staff of service organizations, parks and recreation employees, mothers, fathers, uncles, aunts, and grandparents to be agents talking about their libraries' contributions to their lives. Somebody else besides a few proactive library professionals needs to carry the message that libraries are important—and need adequate funding to carry on their important community responsibilities.

OCLC: WHAT IS ESSENTIAL FOR LIBRARY FUNDING?

Board members and management teams of most public libraries have a good sense of what "positive points" will play with their users and their voters. A good general guide to what plays with local constituents comes from OCLC, which in 2008 published the results of a survey that examined the sources of support for public libraries and why citizens were willing or unwilling to vote for increased funding for public libraries.

After considerable analysis, the OCLC authors suggest: "Belief that the library is a transformational force in people's lives is directly related to their level of funding support." Here is what OCLC discerns as the eight attributes that make U.S. survey respondents "purposeful supporters" of libraries as "a transformational force in people's lives":[13]

- Helps create who you are.
- Makes you feel good about yourself.
- Allows you to appreciate the beauty in life.
- You come away feeling like you really learned something.
- Fills you with hope and optimism.
- Empowers you.
- Helps you seek truth.
- Serves a serious purpose.

One of the most intriguing aspects of the OCLC study is that those who checked off such attributes were strong supporters of public libraries even though they did not use public libraries. In other words, those who believe that libraries perform essential functions, whether users or not, are the strongest library supporters. Helping solve society's problems, including assisting the poor to enter the economic and social mainstream, is one essential element of library work.

Contrast this OCLC finding with one of our most-told stories about how libraries treat the poor, especially those who are mentally ill. We were on one of our numerous visits to libraries, this one to the main facility of a big-city, multibranch library system that, more than in most cities of similar size, serves an upscale population. Walking into the men's restroom near the entrance, the male part of this book's author duo found a middle-aged man, naked except for his shoes and socks, standing silently staring at a blank tile wall. Being a good library citizen, and with my restroom business finished, I walked to the reference desk and said to one of the women behind the desk, "Ma'am, there's a naked man staring at a wall in the men's restroom." "Oh, my goodness," the staff member replied, as she turned to her colleague behind the desk. "Is he back again?"

We found the naked man in the restroom far less offensive than the librarian's condescending reaction. The relevant question from this experience is this: Does this library actually "serve the poor?" Or does it haphazardly, episodically, and naively put up with them? Thirty minutes later, the naked man remained one of the fixtures in the men's restroom. That, we think, answers the previous rhetorical question.

Poor people, just like rich folks, know when they are being "disrespected," to use a wonderfully apt street word. Does your library "help the poor" with essential library service? Or does it disrespect them by episodic inattention or by putting up with their foibles and personal idiosyncrasies to the detriment of all other users?

Essential change for libraries is not about our permanent role to save civilization or about transforming our reading rooms into quiet sanctuaries for worship of the book. Neither is it about how nice librarians allow a naked man demonstrating traits of probable mental illness to stare aimlessly at a restroom wall without being bothered. Rather, it is about what OCLC calls purposeful transformation. It is about what the St. Louis library's board chose to call "organizing library services to improve individual, family and community life."

All public libraries as a matter of institutional policy need to decide how they are going to work with their constituents in these tense times. Library treatment of the poor is an essential effort on which a library's significance as an institution is being or will come to be judged by all of its users and by its funders.

Does your library play an essential role or roles in the lives of the poor in your community? If it does, how do those roles need to be enhanced or changed? If your library plays an ambivalent role or roles, if you and your staff decide it does not perform essential services, what should you do? What you decide to do and to communicate sets the essential quality of how your funders will regard your institution and your professional demeanor both now and in the future.

Notes

1. Adele M. Fasick and Leslie E. Holt, *Managing Children's Services in the Public Library,* 3rd ed. (Westport, Conn.: Libraries Unlimited, 2008), 208.
2. The toolkit is downloadable in PDF from www.librariesincommunities.ca/resources/Community-Led_Libraries_Toolkit.pdf.
3. Kathleen de la Peña McCook, *A Place at the Table* (Chicago: American Library Association, 2000), 10.
4. Available from the Office of Literacy and Outreach Services at www.ala.org/ala/aboutala/offices/olos/toolkits.cfm.
5. "CURL Studies Shift in Homeless Population," *Loyola, The Magazine of Loyola University Chicago,* Summer 2009, www.luc.edu/loyolamagazine/winter08/CURL.html.
6. Michael Daehn, *Marketing the Church: How to Communicate Your Church's Purpose and Passion in a Modern Context* (St. Louis: published by the author, 2006), 187.
7. Ibid., 21.
8. Ibid., 41–67.
9. Sara Laughlin and Ray W. Wilson, *The Quality Library: A Guide to Self-Improvement, Better Efficiency, and Happier Customers* (Chicago: American Library Association, 2008).
10. Joseph R. Matthews, *The Evaluation and Measurement of Library Services* (Westport, Conn.: Libraries Unlimited, 2007).
11. Edmund A. Rossman, *Castles against Ignorance: How to Make Libraries Great Educational Environments* (published by the author, 2006).

12. Gwendolyn Mink and Alice O'Connor, *Poverty in the United States: An Encyclopedia of History, Politics and Policy* (Santa Barbara, Calif.: ABC-CLIO, 2004).

13. Online Computer Library Center, "From Awareness to Funding: A Study of Library Support in America" (2008), www.oclc.org/us/en/reports/funding/default.htm. For a critique of the statistical methods in this report, see Ray Lyons, "Critiquing Advocacy Research Findings: An Illustration from the OCLC Report . . . ," *Public Library Quarterly* 28, no. 3 (2009): 212–226.

Index

You may also be interested in

Public Libraries Going Green: This is the first book to focus strictly on the library's role in going green, helping you with collection development, disposal, and recycling issues; green equipment, technology, and facilities; programming ideas; ways to get the community involved in the process; and more.

Urban Teens in the Library: Based on expert research into the habits and preferences of urban teens, this book offers new and proven ideas for reaching out to them by understanding the value of street lit and social networking, the importance of revamping library services, and much more.

Assessing Service Quality, Second Edition: This classic book is brought fully up to date as Peter Hernon and Ellen Altman integrate the use of technology into the customer experience. Senior librarians, library directors, and trustees will learn how to see the library as the customer does with the aid of dozens of tools to measure service quality—from mystery shoppers and benchmarking to surveys and group interviews.

Boomers and Beyond: A roadmap to trends in and perspectives on the library's role in meeting the needs of our aging population, this book offers proactive ideas that serve the increasing longevity of your patrons, different perspectives on longevity from a variety of scholars and experts, and a section on librarians' responses to the issues.